THE VOICE OF A GIANT

Essays on Seven Russian Prose Classics

edited by

ROGER COCKRELL and DAVID RICHARDS

UNIVERSITY OF EXETER
1985

First published 1985 by the University of Exeter
© 1985 Department of Russian
University of Exeter
ISBN 0 85989 241 7

Printed & bound in Great Britain by
A. Wheaton & Co. Ltd., Exeter

CONTRIBUTORS

A.D.P. Briggs, Reader in Russian Studies, University of Bristol
C.R.S. Cockrell, Lecturer in Russian, University of Exeter
Malcolm V. Jones, Professor of Slavonic Studies, University of Nottingham
W.J. Leatherbarrow, Lecturer in Russian, University of Sheffield
R.A. Peace, Professor of Russian Studies, University of Bristol
D.J. Richards, Reader in Russian, University of Exeter

CONTENTS

PREFACE

The essays in this volume, each by a well-known British scholar, examine seven major prose works of Russian nineteenth-century literature by the leading writers of that era — Pushkin, Lermontov, Gogol, Turgenev, Dostoevsky, Tolstoy and Chekhov.

Every one of these essays began its life as a talk in the *Russian Studies* series of *Exeter Tapes*, a collection of recordings about the language, literature and civilisation of various countries issued by the Language Centre of the University of Exeter. For publication in book form the texts of the seven original talks have been revised — in places quite substantially — and detailed references have been added, together with suggestions for further reading and a list of recommended English translations of the Russian works.

Like the *Exeter Tapes* talks themselves, the present essays aim to be clear and straightforward in their approach, but also intellectually stimulating. They are intended primarily for A-level students of Russian and for first- and second-year undergraduates. At the same time we also hope that they will be of interest to both the general reader and students of literature with no knowledge of the Russian language.

Although they were produced separately, taken together these essays provide a broad impression of Russian nineteenth-century prose fiction, from its beginnings in the 1830s and 1840s with Pushkin, Lermontov and Gogol, through the three great mid-century novelists, Turgenev, Dostoevsky and Tolstoy, to Chekhov, whose *Lady with the Dog*, the final work discussed in the present volume, was published in 1899.

The essays naturally bring out many of the general characteristics of Russian nineteenth-century literature, since it is evident that in spite of their distinctly individual stances the seven authors treated here share many features in common.

In the first place, they are all writing within the context of nineteenth-century Russia which was, by European standards, very backward economically, socially, politically and culturally. In the early years of the century, apart from a handful of wealthy, largely

French-educated aristocrats, the population was poor and benighted; the bulk of the people were peasants — mostly serfs — working on the land; political power rested officially in the absolute authority of the tsar, but was shared in practice between the autocrat and the minute upper class; there was no middle class in the European sense of the word, and few people received any formal education. Even at the end of the century, when the serfs had been emancipated, industrialisation had advanced and various administrative reforms had been enacted, Russia was still decades behind Western Europe and the United States, and literature remained the province of a tiny élite.

That province, however, enjoyed an influence far in excess of its apparent size. Throughout much of the nineteenth century literature was one of the few forums in Russia for relatively free discussion and came to play a key role in the intellectual life of the country. 'Only in literature,' wrote Belinsky in 1847 in his famous letter to Gogol, 'is there still life and progress. That is why the writer's calling is so respected in our country.' Indeed, especially from the middle of the century onwards, literate Russians tended to regard their writers as sages, as men endowed with superior insight into the nature of reality and as spokesmen for spiritual and ethical values. Writers themselves were usually very conscious of their responsibility to society and took this obligation rather more seriously than did most of their counterparts in other countries.

Secondly, the seven writers treated in this volume are all, broadly speaking, literary realists. Their works are firmly anchored in (usually contemporary) nineteenth-century Russia and reflect with a high degree of accuracy the manners, morals and preoccupations of the day. The action of *The Queen of Spades*, *The Greatcoat* and *Notes from Underground* takes place in St Petersburg, *A Hero of Our Time*, *Fathers and Sons* and *The Lady with the Dog* are set in the provinces, while in *War and Peace* Tolstoy takes the reader all over Russia and to various parts of Western Europe as well. In these works we see how nineteenth-century Russians of all classes and conditions dressed, arranged their homes and organised their daily lives; we are shown the relationships between the classes, the generations and the sexes; we learn what they thought about almost everything, from history to hunting, and from letter-writing to the meaning of life; there are descriptions of the seasons and accounts of festivals, ceremonies and entertainments; we can find out what books nineteenth-century Russians read, what travelling was like, when meals were taken, or how duels were fought. For historians and sociologists Russian nineteenth-century literature provides an astonishingly rich fund of information.

At the same time, every one of our authors is much more than a simple archivist or historian of manners. The raw material of Russian life is moulded into coherent works of art which powerfully reflect the personality of the author and his attitude to life. No reader could ever confuse Pushkin's high spirits with Tolstoy's seriousness, Gogol's nightmarish dissonances with Turgenev's harmonious clarity, or Dostoevsky's intensity with Chekhov's light touch.

Furthermore, our authors clearly felt impelled not merely to record the way nineteenth-century Russians acted, thought and felt, but also to analyse these ways and at times to hint at what they considered better or worse attitudes. Running through all the works under discussion — and much more Russian literature besides — is a strong feeling for true and false, worthy and unworthy, or attractive and unattractive behaviour. To that extent every one of these seven works can be regarded as 'moral' — though since moral issues are rarely clear-cut, either in life or in the minds of writers, every work also reflects a large and intriguing measure of doubt and ambiguity. Does Pushkin's sympathy in *The Queen of Spades* go more to the selfish old countess than to her browbeaten ward? Does Lermontov give Pechorin's personal brilliance greater prominence than his moral shortcomings? Is Gurov acting morally or immorally in his adulterous affair with the lady with the dog? Unlikely as it may seem to those brought up in the puritanical traditions of the Russian nineteenth-century civic critics and their modern Soviet successors, the Russian classics are surprisingly undogmatic on such questions.

The seven texts under discussion do not reflect only *moral* ambiguities. A blurring of real life and fantasy lies at the centre of both *The Queen of Spades* and *The Greatcoat;* the question of free will versus determinism is raised in *A Hero of Our Time, Notes from Underground* and *War and Peace;* the last-named novel hints in its very title at two contrasting sides of life; while a central theme of *The Lady with the Dog* is the conflicting claims of the real and the ideal. Again the author rarely commits himself unreservedly to one position rather than the other. As Chekhov once put it in a letter to his publisher, Suvorin (27 October, 1888): 'When you insist that the artist adopt an intelligent attitude towards his work, you are right, but you confuse two things — solving a problem and correctly setting out a problem. Only the latter is obligatory for the artist.' This sensitive and serious open-mindedness is one of the features which has always made the great works of Russian nineteenth-century literature attractive and relevant to readers in all civilised countries of the world.

When those works were first widely reproduced in English during the first two decades of the present century readers and critics alike were struck, perhaps above all else, by the energy which appeared to radiate from the pages, even in translation. Russian authors spoke, it seemed, with a passion and a power which English literature no longer possessed; they ranged more broadly and with a greater concern over human experience and plumbed more readily and with sharper insight the depths of man's psyche; they viewed and depicted life with an unexpected directness and vigour. William Lyon Phelps, an early twentieth-century

American devotee of Russian literature, expressed the general response
when he wrote in his *Essays on Russian Novelists* (1911):

> Russian literature is the voice of a giant, waking from a long sleep,
> and becoming articulate. It is as though the world had watched this
> giant's deep slumber for a long time, wondering what he would say
> when he awakened. And what he has said has been well worth the
> thousand years of waiting.

'The voice of a giant.' Today, more than seventy years later, Phelps'
image still accurately reflects the impression which Russian nineteenth-
century fiction makes on countless English-speaking readers coming to it
for the first time. We hope that the essays in the present volume will help
such readers approach with confidence seven of the most characteristic of
these masterpieces.

Our thanks go to the contributors to this volume for allowing us to
reproduce their Exeter Tapes talks in printed form, to the Publications
Committee of the University of Exeter for their financial support, and to
our secretary, Mrs Lorna Forrest for her abiding patience and dedication.

Note: Every effort has been made to trace the copyright holders of the
photographs reprinted in this book. We apologise for any inadvertent
omission, which can be rectified in a subsequent reprint.

UNIVERSITY OF EXETER   D.R.
October 1984   R.C.

I

PUSHKIN: THE QUEEN OF SPADES

Pushkin's literary status is beyond question for Russians and for those in the West who read Russian. He is 'the father of Russian literature', a remarkable genius directly responsible for the impressive development of Russian literature in the nineteenth century. He is also revered as Russia's finest poet.

But Pushkin's genius — both as artist and as instigator — is by no means as apparent to the casual non-Russian reader, who perhaps has little difficulty in appreciating other Russian writers, such as Dostoevsky, Turgenev and Tolstoy. This certainly was the case with as intelligent and sensitive a reader as Matthew Arnold, who as late as 1887, some 50 years after Pushkin's death, commented that Russia had not yet produced a great poet.[1]

The reason for this view is not difficult to find. Poetry is, in general, very difficult to translate successfully, and this is particularly true of Pushkin's poetry. Therefore, the reader who wisely avoids the largely unsuccessful attempts to render Pushkin's verse in English has no alternative but to base his assessment of Pushkin on the poet's prose, which has been translated more effectively than his verse.[2]

Pushkin was a poet by temperament rather than by choice. His thoughts found their most natural expression in verse, and his adoption of prose towards the end of his short life in many ways ran counter to his nature. As Mirsky suggests, prose for Pushkin was a foreign language which had to be learned, and his use of it, although skilful, is nonetheless deliberate and self-conscious.[3] Puskin's prose never quite conceals his natural tendency to write poetry and we can detect the poet in the very phrasing and tempo of his prose.

Judging Pushkin, therefore, on the strength of his prose is rather like judging Turgenev on the strength of his verse. With the exception of *The Queen of Spades*, Pushkin's achievements in prose are not comparable to his achievements in verse. Neither are tales such as *Dubrovsky*, *The Captain's Daughter* and *The Negro of Peter the Great* likely to find enthusiastic admirers — as distinct from merely respectful ones — among modern readers familiar with the great prose achievements of Pushkin's successors.

But the failure of Pushkin's prose to affect the modern reader to the same extent as does that of, say, Dostoevsky in no way detracts from its

1

A.S. Pushkin 1799-1837

immense historical significance. For without the examples of Pushkin's prose experiments on the one hand, and his novel in verse, *Eugene Onegin*, on the other, it is difficult to believe that the Russian novel would have flourished as it did in the half century following the poet's death.

Pushkin represented the culmination of a great age of Russian poetry. From the reign of Catherine the Great to that of Nicholas I, poetry had been the dominant literary genre, served by writers of outstanding talent and originality, such as Gavriil Derzhavin (1743-1816) and Vasilii Zhukovsky (1783-1852), as well as by a host of lesser figures. Imaginative prose *fiction*, as distinct from the historical works and travel sketches of Nikolai Karamzin (1766–1826), was largely unpractised. Most of the novels read during Pushkin's time were either French or quite unoriginal imitations of French models. There was no tradition of the Russian novel as such, and this point is made with delightful irony in *The Queen of Spades* when Tomsky offers to bring his grandmother a Russian novel and the old Countess replies: 'Are there any Russian novels?'[4]

The only major literary figure who had made a consistent attempt to establish a truly Russian prose fiction was Karamzin, whose mawkishly sentimental tale *Poor Liza*, written in 1792, enjoyed a marked popularity amongst the Russian reading public. Karamzin had made an attempt, which was vigorously resisted by conservative literary figures, to liberate the Russian literary language from the ponderous archaisms of Old Church Slavonic. This he did by bringing it closer to the speech of the educated nobility. Indeed Karamzin's prose was the best Russia had to offer before Pushkin but, as Pushkin himself remarked in 1822: 'That is no great praise'.[5]

Poor Liza has many obvious faults. Apart from its cloyingly sentimental plot about the suicide of a young serf-girl deceived by a thoughtless aristocrat, it is burdened by a wearisome, pretentious and totally unsuitable narrative manner. Purple passages give way to excessively emotional authorial interjections, which in turn yield to quite unconvincing dialogue. Karamzin was bound by literary conventions which did not allow for the straightforward, direct and realistic telling of a tale. Liza's speech — educated and formal — belies her lowly station in life. Peasant girls never spoke in this way, but Karamzin obviously considered it out of the question to introduce the vulgarisms of popular speech into a literature directed exclusively at an educated aristocratic élite.

In sum, everything about *Poor Liza* is excessive and artificial — a long way from the directness and simplicity of Pushkin's own prose manner. And herein lies the true significance of Pushkin's adoption of prose. In his first completed prose work, *The Tales of Belkin*, Pushkin experimented with existing narrative forms and conventions, adapting, testing, and even parodying them; in the process he created a versatile narrative medium —

the first successful Russian prose style — which was to point the way and enable the great age of the Russian realistic novel to follow the golden age of poetry.

This achievement is all the more remarkable if we remember that prose did not come as naturally to Pushkin as poetry and that, with the exception of *The Queen of Spades*, Pushkin's prose lacks the sparkling vitality of his verse. Indeed, in the early part of his career Pushkin was openly contemptuous of prose. 'The thought of prose makes me sick', he wrote in 1823,[6] and in view of the quality of prose written at the time we can perhaps understand his feelings. But fashions in literature change and the popularity of poetry had begun to decline by the end of the reign of Alexander I. Even Pushkin was no longer read as eagerly by a public that now craved prose. He was never a writer who pandered to public opinion, and poems such as *The Poet and the Crowd* (1828) and *To the Poet* (1830) demonstrate his disdain for the opinion of what he called 'the rabble', but it is notable that Pushkin's interest in prose should be awakened at a time when poetry was in decline. After all, he was the first Russian professional writer who relied for his livelihood on selling his manuscripts. Perhaps also he was fascinated by the possibilities of an unfamiliar medium.

By the time he turned to prose Pushkin had for some years been engaged in writing a novel, his masterpiece *Eugene Onegin*, which was not completed until 1830. But *Eugene Onegin* is written in verse and this makes, in Pushkin's words, 'the devil of a difference'.[7] It is quite unlike anything he wrote in prose despite its claim to being a novel. It has none of the studied austerity of his prose manner, but all of the wit and vivacity which characterise his best poetry. It is perhaps the fullest expression of Pushkin's poetic nature.

In all his best works Pushkin maintains an effective interplay between his material and his personality. Everything he wrote in verse bears the stamp of his temperament, but not in an obtrusive fashion as is the case with Tolstoy and Dostoevsky, who constantly force points of view upon their readers. Pushkin keeps company with his reader, not as a teacher or guide, but as an intelligent, witty and sensitive companion who, like the reader, is sufficiently detached from the themes, plots and characters of his works to be able to share his impressions, his delight, his amusement, his irony, and even at times his sadness. *Eugene Onegin* is the supreme example of this kind of work. It is a highly personal piece in which Pushkin mixes the formal elements of the prose novel (plot, characterisation, etc.) with an extensive yet controlled poetic self-display. Pushkin is the commanding presence in the work. He interrupts, digresses, comments and reminisces; and in the process he grafts onto the novel a rich additional subjective world.

If poetry and 'the novel in verse' offered Pushkin the means for this delightful self-display, prose afforded him the opportunity of trying something quite different which ran against the grain of his nature — narrative impersonality. The reader is struck immediately by the directness of Pushkin's prose style. His tales are above all action stories, where the plot is promoted at the expense of description, digression, dialogue and analysis. In Pushkin's prose, unlike his poetry, the narrator usually plays an essentially passive role. This is particularly obvious in *The Tales of Belkin*, where Pushkin employs several narrators in order to maintain a distance between the characters and situations described in the tales and the real narrator — himself.

This approach may be compared with that of Pushkin's contemporary, Nikolai Gogol, whose stories are showcases for an obtrusive storyteller. Pushkin viewed prose quite differently from Gogol. He also saw it as a method quite distinct from poetry as it allowed for a totally impersonal narrative. Ironically enough, it might well have been the writing of the capricious and highly personal *Eugene Onegin* that fully revealed to Pushkin the possibilities offered by prose. Certainly, in a well-known passage from Chapter III of the work Pushkin anticipates eventually abandoning poetry for 'humble prose'.[8] In his novel in verse Pushkin had for the first time tried his hand at an extended plot, extended characterisation and a detailed evocation of a certain class of Russian life. As Pushkin no doubt saw, prose is the medium best suited to a work of this type and this scale, and *Eugene Onegin* remains the only successful Russian novel in verse. The subsequent great Russian novels, although often relying upon characters and situations deriving from Pushkin's work, were written in prose. It is ironic, however, that few Russian novelists inherited Pushkin's view of prose as an impersonal narrative medium. The nineteenth-century Russian novel was to become the vehicle for the propagation of opinion and personal views.

Pushkin's first major prose attempt was *The Negro of Peter the Great*, written in 1827 after he had been reading the historical romances of Walter Scott. Like the works of Scott, *The Negro of Peter the Great* aims to evoke a distinct historical period, but unlike Scott's novels it is written in the terse and economic prose so characteristic of Pushkin. Significantly, it is unfinished. Many of Pushkin's prose works were left uncompleted, which suggests perhaps that they were seen by him essentially as experimental pieces rather than as independent works of art.

Pushkin did not turn to prose in earnest until 1830, shortly before his marriage. He had travelled to his father's estate at Boldino, which he was due to receive as a wedding present, and stayed there for most of the autumn because of an outbreak of cholera. This period of isolation at Boldino was the most intensely creative period of Pushkin's life. While there he completed *Eugene Onegin*, composed his *Little Tragedies*, and wrote the collection of stories entitled *The Tales of Belkin*. *The Queen of Spades* was written during a second, brief Boldino autumn in 1833.

As early as 1822 Pushkin had drafted an article in which he considered
the principles of prose. Like so much of Pushkin's prose fiction, this
article remained unfinished, but enough of it exists to show that Pushkin
valued precision and brevity as the cardinal virtues of prose. In one
passage he scathingly dismisses those writers who burden narrative with
rhetoric:

> What are we to say of our writers who, considering it beneath them to
> write simply of ordinary things, think to liven up their childish prose
> with embellishments and faded metaphors? These people can never
> say *friendship* without adding 'that sacred sentiment whose noble
> flame, etc.' They should be saying 'early in the morning', but they
> write: 'Hardly had the first rays of the rising sun illumined the eastern
> edge of the azure sky...' Oh! How new and fresh this all is! Is it any
> the better just because it is longer?[9]

In *The Queen of Spades* Pushkin puts his early ideas on prose most
effectively into practice. It is a very short work, with a very simple plot, a
handful of characters and no obvious message or rich passages of
description. And yet it echoes in the mind like few other works, and lends
itself to the sort of detailed analysis that critics usually reserve for much
longer pieces. The virtues of precision and brevity are in evidence
throughout the work, in its characterisation, its plot and its narrative style.

In his presentation of the characters, for example, Pushkin ignores the
obvious ways of making a character memorable, such as detailed physical
description, lengthy dialogue and thumbnail sketches of personal history
or cast of mind. Instead he creates quite distinct images with the minimum
use of words. His secret is quite simple, if difficult to emulate. Rather than
give his reader masses of information in the hope that the really
memorable and significant details are included somewhere, Pushkin
selects only those details which are evocative enough to allow the reader to
complete the picture in his mind. For example, the gambler Chekalinsky
is perfectly sketched in only ten or so lines:

> He was a man of about 60, of most respectable appearance. His head
> was covered with silvery grey hair; his full, fresh face expressed good
> humour; his eyes glittered, enlivened by a perpetual smile. Narumov
> introduced Hermann to him. Chekalinsky shook his hand cordially,
> asked him not to stand on ceremony and continued dealing...

> Chekalinsky paused after every round to give the players time to
> arrange their cards and note their losses, listened courteously to their
> requests and more courteously still straightened the corner of a card
> which some thoughtless hand had folded over.[10]

How vividly Chekalinsky is depicted here, with his intelligence, his good nature, his charm and, not least, his tact in quietly passing over the 'thoughtless hand's' attempt to cheat by doubling a stake after the game had been played.

Pushkin is equally effortless and economical in presenting his hero, Hermann, who comes to life through a few simple leitmotifs which Pushkin repeats at intervals throughout the tale, as he would in a poem. These include Hermann's German origins, which would have been enough to render him ridiculous in the eyes of Pushkin's French-educated contemporaries, and his passionate commitment to gambling together with an unwillingness 'to risk the necessary in the hope of gaining the superfluous', which mark him out as a hopelessly split personality and anticipate his madness.

Pushkin is careful also in his deployment of the plot. Nothing is allowed to detract from the purposeful account of Hermann's descent from moderation to incarceration. This overriding concern for action makes *The Queen of Spades* a superb mystery story, and Mirsky comments that it 'is as tense as a compressed spring'.[11] The reader is caught up in the tempo of the work, and this tempo is never relaxed by digressions, descriptions and lengthy dialogues. Minimum use is made of adjectives and adverbs that might inhibit the flow of action.

Yet despite the apparent thinness of both Pushkin's scene-setting and his characters' dialogue, these are never less than totally convincing. Unlike Karamzin's Liza, Pushkin's characters speak as one might expect people of their kind to speak: Hermann, in the conventional clipped manner of a cautious German; the old Countess, in the dignified but slightly archaic manner of a living relic. Similarly, Pushkin sets his scenes with the brevity of a dramatist's stage directions, but the richness and authority of a novelist. The short opening paragraph conveys a wealth of important information:

> Once they were playing cards in the rooms of Narumov, a Guards Officer. The long winter night had passed unnoticed, and they only sat down to supper about five in the morning. Those who had won ate with great appetite; the rest, in distraction, sat before their empty plates. But the champagne appeared, the conversation picked up, and all took part in it.[12]

How suggestive even the simplest words are. For instance, Pushkin does not need to describe who *they* (the cardplayers) are, for who but the privileged classes can afford to take supper at 5 a.m.? Likewise, the feverish compulsion of gambling is communicated by the short phrase: 'The long winter night had passed unnoticed'. The single adverb *unnoticed* (*nezametno*) eloquently conveys the dedication of the participants.

By writing in this fashion Pushkin is able to convey a great deal in a very short space. By the end of the first page of the tale the scene has been set, both physically and socially, and the reader has been introduced to all the major characters (except Lizaveta Ivanovna), the tale of the mysterious cards, and the hero's tragically split nature.

In this way Pushkin demonstrates that denseness of language is unnecessary. A single word, provided it is the right word, can speak volumes. This is why *The Queen of Spades*, a short mystery story, raises as many questions in the reader's mind as a much longer work.

———————

The Queen of Spades may come as a surprise to modern readers familiar with the work of other nineteenth-century Russian prose writers. It does not appear to provide those features expected in a masterpiece of Russian literature. It is by any standards brief, but particularly so in contrast with the immense novels of Tolstoy and Dostoevsky with which the term 'Russian literature' is usually associated in the West. Moreover, *The Queen of Spades* is, as we have seen, primarily an *action* story, uncluttered by the pages of philosophical and religious speculation which are recognised as another of Russian literature's hallmarks. Pushkin's tale contains no tortured intellectuals speculating about the meaning of life and death or repentant noblemen abandoning corrupt society for a more direct and meaningful life among peasants or cossacks. It appears to be a simple society tale, laced with a dash of the supernatural, which offers no obvious message or revelation.

It is not only modern readers who have been struck by the apparent slightness of *The Queen of Spades*. Although it gained an immediate popularity amongst the reading public in Russia, the Russian literary critics of the 1840s and 1850s, who were for the most part also social critics, found very little in the tale to write about. Men such as Vissarion Belinsky in the 1840s and Nikolai Chernyshevsky in the 1850s saw literature as a potentially powerful weapon in the struggle for social and political change. To readers of such outlook *The Queen of Spades* offered little. Belinsky was clearly embarrassed by the tale's exclusiveness — it was obviously written to be read with pleasure by readers of Pushkin's own society, the privileged and educated classes. Similarly, Chernyshevsky found many of Pushkin's works well-written but essentially slight.

Temperamentally, if not chronologically, Pushkin was an eighteenth-century aristocratic man of letters, whose works, in their elegance, precision and polish, reflect the conviction that art, if it is not well-executed, is nothing at all. His mature view of art was uncompromisingly aesthetic. 'The aim of poetry is poetry', he once wrote,[13] and he could not look upon literature as a work-horse condemned to draw intolerably heavy philosophical and moral burdens. This is not to suggest that Pushkin did not take literature seriously; on the contrary, he believed that poetic inspiration was divine. It is simply that Pushkin's seriousness and commitment to literature were of a different kind from those of his successors; literature could be serious without being grave, and it could uplift without instructing. Pushkin wore the mantle of the artist lightly and elegantly, but this same mantle was to prove too cumbersome for many of his followers.

In his social attitudes too Pushkin differed from later Russian writers, and this is worth examining because throughout the history of literature the writer's social outlook has largely conditioned his view of art. The guilt, for example, which Tolstoy felt on behalf of his social class, the nobility, is central to the development of his writing and to his rejection of 'sophisticated' literature in favour of simpler forms accessible to the ordinary working people.

Pushkin was rarely inconvenienced by democratic leanings. He was the product of an established Europeanised aristocratic society, and inordinately proud of his own 600-year-old lineage. He regarded the nobility, and by implication the idea of social privilege, as 'a necessary and natural feature of a great civilised nation'.[14] He was an élitist and a snob, and these characteristics are quite obvious in his work. He addressed himself for the most part to his social equals and had little time for those who were unwilling or unable to appreciate the sophistication of his genius. Of course it was far easier for Pushkin to maintain this attitude than it would have been for Tolstoy. Pushkin lived and wrote towards the end of a great age of the nobility in Russia. Democratic and populist attitudes existed, but were nothing like as widespread or as fashionable as they were to become later in the nineteenth century, following the development in Russia of a mixed-class, as opposed to exclusively aristocratic intelligentsia.

Values have of course changed since Pushkin's day, and attitudes and assumptions regarded then as natural and unquestionable may now appear to be decadent, frivolous, unfair and irresponsible. Perhaps this is why *The Queen of Spades* fails to satisfy the literary taste of many modern readers, and here 'modern' can mean not just ourselves, but also people as close chronologically to Pushkin as Belinsky and Chernyshevsky, who had come to expect more from literature than a simple society tale. In short, *The Queen of Spades* is not likely to evoke widespread admiration today because it is, in a modern context, aristocratically unfair, provocatively amoral and intellectually lightweight. It cannot be described as 'a vivid exposé of a corrupt society', or 'an urgent analysis of the ethical problems facing us all', etc.

Many details of *The Queen of Spades* locate it firmly in a bygone age. For example, the story's exclusiveness has already been mentioned. It is directed unambiguously at a tiny, privileged section of nineteenth-century Russian society. One suspects that it would have meant little to people of lesser status, even to those capable of reading, for the reader is expected to grasp and appreciate references and attitudes familiar only to polite society. Apart from making allusions to contemporary society, figures and events, which the hypothetical middle-class reader of the time might conceivably have been able to trace, Pushkin assumes familiarity on his reader's part with manners, customs and attitudes practised only by the upper reaches of society.[15] The reader is expected, for example, to respond immediately and in the right way to the distinction drawn by society between Hermann's status, that of an engineer, and Narumov's, that of a guardsman. Only then can he understand the suggestiveness of Tomsky's incredulity when the socially naive Lizaveta Ivanovna implies that the immaculately well-bred Narumov might be a mere engineer.

But in a more general sense Pushkin assumes that the intelligence and outlook of the reader are comparable to his own. For example, he takes it for granted that his reader will be able to play with ideas and concepts as easily and naturally as he does. For Pushkin such playfulness was second nature. He was able to juggle even with serious concepts without either being enslaved by them or rendering them ridiculous. A tone of playfulness and the skilful use of parody are central to *The Queen of Spades*, and their presence effectively deters the reader from interpreting the tale too seriously. Whoever draws heavy social or moral conclusions from this work is guilty of a gross failure of response.

The Queen of Spades is rich in literary allusions and echoes which would have been quite apparent to Pushkin's contemporaries. The whole tale is built around the juxtaposition of features characteristic of two literary genres popular at the time: the gothic tale of the supernatural, and the realistic social and psychological sketch. Pushkin assumes his reader's familiarity with these two forms and then proceeds to hold their seemingly contradictory demands together for the duration of his tale. As a result, the reader is never sure whether he is dealing with a work of fantasy or a work of psychological realism. The opening of *The Queen of Spades* skilfully establishes the ambiguity: the epigraph and Tomsky's introduction of the story of the mysterious card trick both speak clearly of supernatural forces awaiting the ambitious Hermann, but at the same time the reader learns of Hermann's hopelessly split nature, torn between the extremes of sobriety and wild imagination. Either could account for his eventual downfall. Likewise, the reader is made to feel uneasy about Pushkin's immaculately realistic depiction of upper-class Russian life by the occasional references to real people with mysterious associations, such as the strange Count Saint-Germain, who had revealed the secret of the cards to the old Countess.

Ambiguity informs the whole work. Is Hermann the victim of a supernatural conspiracy which avenges his abuse of Lizaveta Ivanovna and the death of the Countess? Or is he simply a mad German whose amply demonstrated imagination accounts for his apparently supernatural downfall? Pushkin allows both possibilities, and the uncertainty is skilfully reinforced in the following extract:

> Hermann was the son of a Russified German, who had left him a small capital sum. Being firmly convinced of the need to consolidate his independence, Hermann did not touch even the interest, but lived on his salary, denying himself even the slightest extravagance. Moreover, he was reserved and ambitious, so that his companions rarely had the opportunity to make fun of his excessive thrift. He had strong passions and an ardent imagination, but his resoluteness saved him from the customary indiscretions of youth. Thus, for instance, although he was a gambler at heart, he never touched cards, for he reckoned that his circumstances did not allow him (as he put it) 'to risk the necessary in the hope of gaining the superfluous'. Yet despite this he spent whole nights sitting at the card tables, following with feverish excitement the vicissitudes of the game.
>
> The tale of the thre cards had had a powerful effect on Hermann's imagination and preyed on his mind the whole night. 'What if,' he thought to himself the next evening as he wandered around St Petersburg, 'What if the old Countess were to reveal her secret to me? Or tell me the three lucky cards? Why shouldn't I try my luck?... I could get introduced to her, win her favour, perhaps even become her lover. But that would all take time, and she is eighty-seven. She could be dead within a week, or even a couple of days! And what about the tale itself? Can one believe it?... No, economy, moderation and hard work — these are my three lucky cards. They will treble my capital, increase it sevenfold and bring me leisure and independence!'[16]

On one level of this passage a strong case is made out for a realistic interpretation of subsequent events. We are told, for example, that Hermann 'had strong passions and an ardent imagination, but his resoluteness saved him from the customary indiscretions of youth'; that he was 'a gambler at heart', but had 'never touched cards' and that he followed each game 'with feverish excitement'. These brief psychological brushstrokes point unmistakeably to a man whose moderate veneer only just restrains a wild and imaginative nature. This interpretation is given added weight by Hermann's rapid and extreme psychological fluctuations, as for example when he dreams wildly one moment of becoming the Countess' lover, only to be brought immediately down to earth by the sobering thought that she is eighty-seven years old. As a result of this thought Hermann decides to dismiss his thirst for the secret of the card trick and resolves: 'Economy, moderation and hard work — these are my three lucky cards', which will 'treble my capital, increase it sevenfold...'. The numbers Hermann hits upon here are significant, for the Three, the Seven and the Ace are the cards to be revealed to him later by the Countess' ghost. Pushkin is evidently suggesting that the numbers are for some reason already fixed in Hermann's mind and that he simply imagines the Countess' subsequent visitation.

At this point in the chapter the realistic interpretation has the upper hand, but Pushkin goes on to cloud the issue and resurrect the possibility of supernatural intervention. During his walk home Hermann suddenly finds himself before a large house. His enquiries reveal that this is none other than the house of the Countess whose history has so occupied his imagination. Coincidence, perhaps? He resumes his wanderings, but then again suddenly finds himself before the same house. Coincidence becomes less likely, and, like Hermann, the reader suspects the existence of some unknown force directing his steps.

There are many other instances of such ambiguity. It is not clear that Hermann really sees the Countess' corpse wink at him: Pushkin's use of the phrase 'it seemed to him' keeps the issue open.[17] Neither are we sure that he really sees the ghost; we are told before this 'visit' that Hermann can think of nothing but the death of the Countess and that 'contrary to his custom he had drunk a great deal'.[18]

Pushkin's emphasis upon such playful ambiguity is achieved perhaps at the expense of the more serious implications of a story about greed, ambition and murder, but certainly not at the expense of its entertainment value. And Pushkin's desire to entertain rather than instruct is one of the features which clearly distinguish him from later Russian writers.

We see the entertainer/parodist at work again in the choice of characters for the tale. All of them are literary stereotypes common in works of the time, and were therefore as familiar to Pushkin's contemporaries as they are today. But Pushkin does not give his reader what he has come to expect from such characters. He compels him instead to regard familiar figures in a new light. The reader of popular sentimental or sensational tales might well expect to respond to the conventional figures of the Countess, Lizaveta Ivanovna and Hermann in certain well-defined ways. The old Countess, for example, is the familiar tyrant/villain figure and might be expected to arouse in the reader distaste for her obvious unfairness and selfishness; Lizaveta Ivanovna, the archetypal sentimental heroine/victim, should engender compassion; and Hermann, the stock romantic hero of melodrama, admiration for his strength of will. After all, he is the man of the future, trying to establish himself by manipulating the injustices of a vanishing way of life.

But these conventional reactions are not the ones Pushkin ultimately provokes in his reader. It becomes obvious in the course of the tale that

Pushkin regards his characters not in a moral light, but in an aesthetic one, and the reader is invited to do the same. This distances Pushkin from the moralists who followed him and firmly set the tone of later Russian literature and discloses just how old-fashioned *The Queen of Spades* is. Pushkin's aristocratic self-confidence and his sense of the dignity and stability of his class and its values allow him to evade altogether the moral issues raised by the tale and to judge his characters — for judge them he does, albeit unobtrusively — against aesthetic and class criteria. Thus the self-centred, spiteful and no doubt undeserving Countess receives from Pushkin the tacit approval he withholds from the poor and worthy Lizaveta Ivanovna. Pushkin suggests that you do not have to be good to be appealing, and that style can conceal — indeed, atone for — a multitude of sins. And this wicked old lady certainly has style. Her dubious ethics and swollen legs count for little when we see just how skilled she is at the arts of survival and oneupmanship. She has lived for years with a secret which could make a fortune, but regards it as unimportant; as John Bayley has remarked: 'Class has no need of magic'.[19] She displays a remarkable ability to keep one step ahead of those who surround her. For example, when her grandson, Tomsky, lets slip that the last of the old Countess' contemporaries has passed away, the predictably solicitous Lizaveta Ivanovna tries to soften the news in order to spare the Countess' feelings. What she fails to see is that the old lady, far from being concerned and dispirited, is delighted. She has outdone her contemporaries by outliving them. She delights in attending balls where she is unwanted and where she knows that her presence as a relic of the past inhibits the future. Her stubborn refusal to rest in dignified peace is also entirely in character. There is no doubt that, of all the characters in the tale, she has the lion's share of Pushkin's sympathy.

Pushkin's attitude to Lizaveta Ivanovna is also unexpected. He obviously finds her poor, innocent and humiliated, but, most important of all, she is dull. She has a certain drab righteousness, but no style whatsoever. Pushkin's essentially aesthetic rather than ethical outlook is clear in a passage where, no doubt with the best of intentions, he begins to describe Lizaveta's hardships, but cannot resist transferring his attention from this tediously upright girl to the much more interesting items of furniture which surround her.[20]

The same is true of Hermann. Readers familiar with the character of Rastignac in Balzac's novel, *Le Père Goriot*, published in 1834 soon after *The Queen of Spades*, might see in Hermann a similar romantic, demonic figure. But Hermann is a parody of the romantic man of will, a vulgar and prosaic figure despite his involvement in the death of the Countess. One suspects that Pushkin allows the full weight of retribution to fall upon Hermann, not because he has killed, but because he has done so without style and panache. His real sin is his dullness and the ridiculous figure he

14   *The Voice of a Giant*

cuts when, instead of murdering the Countess with the ruthless resolve of a Napoleon whom he resembles only in profile, he timidly waves an unloaded revolver under her nose and watches her die of fright. The old Countess displays her natural superiority even at the moment of death, by depriving Hermann of heroic stature.

In a world in which ethical considerations often rank higher than aesthetic ones Pushkin's tendency to invert this hierarchy. is unlikely to find general favour. *The Queen of Spades* emphasises Pushkin's distance from present values and has been a particular source of embarrassment for Soviet literary critics who are expected to re-examine the great works of the past in order to emphasise those features which imply a progressive social philosophy. For such reapers *The Queen of Spades* yields a most frustratingly poor harvest.

NOTES

1. Matthew Arnold, *Essays in Criticism* (Second Series), London, 1908, p. 257.
2. Two recent verse translations of Pushkin's novel in verse, *Eugene Onegin* are worthy exceptions. These are by Charles Johnston (Penguin, Harmondsworth, 1979) and Walter Arndt (Dutton, New York, 1981).
3. D. S. Mirsky, *A History of Russian Literature*, Routledge & Kegan Paul, London, 1964, p. 117.
4. A. S. Pushkin, *Polnoe sobranie sochinenii v desyati tomakh*, Leningrad, 1977-79, VI, p. 215.
5. *P.S.S.* VII, p. 13.
6. Letter to P. A. Vyazemsky, 19 August 1823, *P.S.S.*, X, p. 52.
7. Letter to Vyazemsky, 4 November 1823, *P.S.S.*, X, p. 57.
8. *P.S.S.*, V, p. 53.
9. *P.S.S.*, VII, p. 12.
10. *P.S.S.*, VI, p. 235.
11. D. S. Mirsky, p. 119.
12. *P.S.S.*, VI, p. 210.
13. Letter to V.A. Zhukovsky, 20 April 1825, *P.S.S.*, X, p.112.
14. *P.S.S.*, VII, p.136.
15. See J. Bayley, *Pushkin. A Comparative Commentary*, Cambridge University Press, Cambridge, 1971, p.321.
16. *P.S.S.*, VI, pp.218-219.
17. *P.S.S.*, VI, p.232.
18. *P.S.S.*, VI, p.232.
19. Bayley, p.319.
20. *P.S.S.*, VI, p.217.

FURTHER READING ON PUSHKIN

John Bayley, *Pushkin. A Comparative Commentary*, Cambridge University Press, Cambridge, 1971.

A.D.P. Briggs, *Alexander Pushkin. A Critical Study*, Croom Helm, London, 1983.

D.J. Richards and C.R.S. Cockrell, *Russian Views of Pushkin*, Meeuws, Oxford, 1976.

II

LERMONTOV: A HERO OF OUR TIME

Critics nearly always call Lermontov's *A Hero of Our Time* a novel, but in its general shape the work does not conform with the familiar pattern which we see in the traditional English or French nineteenth-century novel from writers such as Stendhal and Balzac, George Eliot and Hardy, or in a Russian work like, say, Turgenev's *Fathers and Sons*. Consider the shape of *Fathers and Sons*. First of all, it has a fairly obvious beginning, middle and end. At the beginning most of the characters are introduced, both to the reader and to each other; in the middle they undergo various experiences, as a result of which they change and develop; and at the end they go their separate, or newly-shared ways. Secondly, in *Fathers and Sons* Turgenev presents the various incidents which make up his story straightforwardly and, for the most part, in chronological order; one event leads clearly on to the next, and at the end everything is neatly tied up. Thirdly, the action is described from the viewpoint of one calm, unbiassed and apparently omniscient narrator, whose tone remains consistent and even from the first page to the last.

Fathers and Sons, however, is in its shape far from a typical nineteenth-century Russian novel, the majority of which do not follow this familiar and seemingly obvious pattern but indeed evince a striking waywardness of form. Pushkin's *Eugene Onegin*, for instance, is written not in prose, but in regular 14-line stanzas. Pushkin himself called his masterpiece 'a novel in verse' (*roman v stikhax*). Gogol's *Dead Souls* is certainly written in prose, but the author dubbed his work 'a narrative poem' (*poema*); it roams and wanders like a great Russian river, but without reaching a goal. Remember Tolstoy's *War and Peace*, which Henry James (who felt more at home with Turgenev) called a 'large, loose and baggy monster', and remember, too, Dostoevsky's *The Brothers Karamazov*, which is almost equally baggy and moreover as unfinished as *Dead Souls*. In this company, it must be admitted, *A Hero of Our Time* appears somewhat less eccentric in its shape than it might elsewhere.

But what is the shape of Lermontov's masterpiece and how does the novel fit together? The most obvious feature is that *A Hero of Our Time* is divided, not into a flowing stream of consecutively numbered chapters, but into seven quite distinct sections. Moreover, these seven sections are presented by four different people: firstly, Lermontov's main fictional narrator, an anonymous traveller, relates the opening two episodes, *Bela*

M. Yu. Lermontov 1814–41

and *Maksim Maksimych*, though one must remember that in *Bela* this
ostensible narrator not only describes his journey through the Caucasus
but also, more importantly, transmits Maksim Maksimych's stories about
Pechorin. Since the latter are given *verbatim*, Maksim Maksimych too
must be included in the list of narrators. The anonymous traveller-
narrator also contributes the explanatory *Foreword to Pechorin's Diary*.
Then, Pechorin himself is the writer of the said diary, which contains the
three episodes *Taman'*, *Princess Mary* and *The Fatalist*. Finally,
Lermontov himself speaks directly to the reader, but only very briefly, in
the *Foreword* to the whole book — a section which was added to the
original text for the second edition of *A Hero of Our Time* in 1841.

Further, the five story-sections of the novel vary quite considerably in
their content and atmosphere: *Bela* presents a combination of travelogue
and romantic adventure tale; *Maksim Maksimych* offers primarily a
character sketch of the kindly Caucasian veteran who exemplifies all the
warm, down-to-earth solidity which Pechorin lacks; *Taman'* is largely a
mystery story; *Princess Mary* contains the bulk of Lermontov's complex
psychological analysis of his hero, while *The Fatalist* is a fascinating
anecdote, laced with a little philosophising. Even the two *Forewords*, the
one to Pechorin's diary and the one which precedes the main text, are not
at all similar. The *Foreword to Pechorin's Diary*, allegedly written by the
anonymous traveller-narrator, gently and straightforwardly praises
Pechorin's sincerity and honest self-analysis, and suggests that he has been
badly misinterpreted by his acquaintances. The *Foreword* to the whole
book, however, which Lermontov wrote in response to some unfavourable
criticism of the novel's first edition of 1840, is far from gentle and
straightforward in its biting irony and defensive aggressiveness.

On top of this, the five story-sections of *A Hero of Our Time* do not
describe Pechorin's experiences in the order in which they happened. The
chronological sequence of events, which can be reconstructed by a close
reading of the text, would seem to be more or less the following:

(1) Pechorin, a young army officer, has been posted to the Caucasus
because of some misdemeanour in St Petersburg. While travelling
south to join his new unit he has to spend a night in the Black Sea port
of Taman', where he clashes with the smugglers in the way described in
the opening episode of his diary, *Taman'*.
(2) After taking part in a few skirmishes with the Caucasian tribesmen,
Pechorin spends a short leave in Pyatigorsk. What happens there is
related in *Princess Mary*.
(3) Because of the duel with Grushnitsky, recorded at the end of the
Princess Mary episode, Pechorin is posted to a frontline fort under the
command of Maksim Maksimych. Here the adventures described in
Bela take place.

(4) While attached to this same fort Pechorin spends a fortnight in a cossack village, where the incidents outlined in *The Fatalist* occur.

(5) About five years later Pechorin (who had resigned his commission shortly after Bela's death) is on his way to Persia. In Vladikavkaz he meets both Lermontov's fictional narrator and Maksim Maksimych.

(6) On the return journey from Persia Pechorin dies. The reader learns of this, however, not at the end of *A Hero of Our Time*, but about one third of the way through, in the anonymous traveller-narrator's *Foreword to Pechorin's Diary*.

Why are the episodes of *A Hero of Our Time* not presented in chronological order? Part of the explanation may derive from the origins of the work, which began its life not as a complete novel, but with the publication of the three pieces, *Bela*, *The Fatalist* and *Taman'* quite separately from each other in the Journal *Notes of the Fatherland* in 1839 and early 1840. But much more crucial were Lermontov's aims. The traditional nineteenth-century novelist usually adopted a chronological approach to his material because he was intent on portraying characters in the process of development. Lermontov however, is not greatly concerned with Pechorin's development; he wants rather to present a psychological analysis of a type of personality or a cast of mind, 'a portrait', as he puts it in his *Foreword* to the novel, 'composed of the vices of our entire generation in their ultimate development'. To this end Lermontov opts to examine the mature Pechorin from a number of different points of view rather than to trace the lines along which he evolved — though references to Pechorin's past are made from time to time.

However, if Lermontov avoids the traditional chronological line of narration, he replaces it with other patterns of movement in *A Hero of Our Time*. For instance, Pechorin is gradually brought closer and closer to the reader. First of all, in *Bela*, he is merely the subject of a long reminiscence narrated by Maksim Maksimych; then, in the episode entitled *Maksim Maksimych*, he appears in person, but only very briefly; then at last he is portrayed much more fully, and inevitably much more sympathetically, through his own diary.

At the same time, the reader's impression of Pechorin's strength of character alternates from episode to episode. In *Bela* he sounds dominating and masterful, but in *Taman'* he seems to be beguiled, outwitted and nearly murdered by the girl-smuggler; then in *Princess Mary* he appears once more to be in command of almost every situation, but at the end, in *The Fatalist*, the very existence of human freedom is called into question, and we are left wondering whether Pechorin — and everyone else too — is perhaps neither strong nor weak, but simply an involuntary puppet controlled by some higher force.

Another interesting line of movement which can be observed is the way the tempo of the narration steadily increases, from Maksim Maksimych's leisurely and oft-interrupted discourse in *Bela* to the dynamic and rapid style adopted by Pechorin himself in *The Fatalist*. Further, the settings of the five story-sections, as they stand, alternate between primitive and civilised. Finally, it is interesting to note how the whole text (disregarding the opening *Foreword*) is framed by the figure of Maksim Maksimych: he is the first of the principal characters to appear and speak (at the beginning of *Bela*) and it is to him that the last spoken words of all also belong (at the end of *The Fatalist*). In such a carefully designed work of art this cannot be simply an accident: Lermontov is presumably indicating that the ordinary, straightforward, good-natured Russians, of whom Maksim Maksimych is a worthy and attractive representative, are much more durable (and perhaps ultimately more valuable) than the brilliant Pechorins of this world.

Another question which must be asked about the order of the episodes is why Lermontov should have chosen to conclude *A Hero of Our Time* with *The Fatalist*? Two reasons immediately suggest themselves. In the first place, he probably did not want to end his novel with Pechorin's death (or even with Grushnitsky's) but rather with an affirmation of Pechorin's positive energy and daring. In the second place, the discussion about fatalism in this concluding section not only sets all the previous action and all the questions about Pechorin's nature against a broader background, but also quite deliberately tries to dissuade the reader from making firm judgments about man's responsibility for his actions and hence from either condemning or exonerating Pechorin for his behaviour. In this connection it is interesting to see how *The Fatalist* re-echoes those notes of hesitation and doubt which are struck in both *Forewords:* the opening *Foreword* ends with the words 'God only knows',[1] and the second with 'I don't know'.[2]

If these lines of movement through the various sections of *A Hero of Our Time* are an important aspect of the novel's general shape, another significant and interesting feature is the way the main characters are arranged. Pechorin is clearly central, even though Lermontov introduces him to the reader tantalisingly slowly at first. Pechorin is the hero referred to in the novel's title; he is the only character to appear in every one of the book's sections, and it is his actions, his thoughts and his psychology which remain the focus of attention throughout. In comparison with Pechorin, all the other characters are of secondary interest; some of them are brilliantly individualised, but they all revolve round Pechorin and serve primarily to highlight facets of his complex and contradictory nature.

Of these figures who circle round Pechorin six are portrayed in considerable detail, a nicely balanced group of three men (Maksim

Maksimych, Dr Werner and Grushnitsky) and three women (Bela, Princess Mary and Vera). The fact that every one of these very different people is drawn to Pechorin emphasises immediately the latter's complexity and wide appeal. More than this, though, each one of these six characters brings out aspects of Pechorin which might otherwise have remained concealed from the reader.

It is worth considering how our view of Pechorin would be defective if one or other of them were absent. Take Werner, for instance, the quick-witted and cynical doctor with whom Pechorin feels such an intellectual affinity. Pechorin's friendship with Werner convinces the reader of two things which he might otherwise have doubted, firstly that Pechorin is genuinely intelligent, and secondly that he is not condemned to be completely isolated from all his fellow-men.

Or look at Vera's role. Her presence in the novel shows that a deep mutual attachment can exist between Pechorin and a sensitive, mature woman. Without Vera we would see Pechorin impressing only rather inexperienced young women. More than this, though, Vera is said to *understand* Pechorin, and in this way Lermontov is able to emphasise that his hero is not necessarily the inscrutable enigma which he seems to be to everybody else. Lermontov exploits Vera's intimate knowledge of Pechorin most effectively at the end of the *Princess Mary* episode, when he has her write a final letter to Pechorin in which she expresses authoritative judgments on various aspects of his character.

Or, to take one more example, what of Grushnitsky? Lermontov may perhaps have feared that his hero might be seen by some readers as little more than a foppish poseur, and one way in which he guards against this interpretation is by introducing the unambiguously empty and affected figure of Grushnitsky, who through his revealed lack of the qualities he affects to possess demonstrates that Pechorin is genuinely confident, sophisticated, courageous and sensitive.

Finally, no discussion of the shape of *A Hero of Our Time* can ignore the unifying role played by Lermontov's language. The remarkably consistent tone maintained from the beginning to the end of the work serves as a fine but immensely strong thread binding the diverse episodes into one whole. By fusing sensitive descriptions with tough-minded, even ruthless analysis Lermontov forges a style which is simultaneously robust and lyrical. It is a style which deliberately and splendidly mirrors the coincident muscular and poetic qualities of Lermontov's principal character, Grigorii Alexandrovich Pechorin, to whom we must now turn.

For the majority of readers the most memorable feature of *A Hero of Our Time* is the figure of Pechorin. His assertive personality provoked heated debates in Russian literary circles when the novel was first published in 1840, and with his singular mixture of almost larger-than-life vices and virtues Lermontov's hero arouses equally strong reactions in the modern reader almost a century and a half later.

Pechorin's vices are obvious. In spite of all the advantages he enjoys of birth, riches, health and intelligence, he is bored with life and disillusioned; he is self-centred and combative, and he acts coldly even towards his friends; worst of all perhaps, he possesses a streak of cruelty. In the well-known entry in his diary for 3rd June he confesses: 'I look upon the sufferings and joys of others only in relation to myself, as nourishment to support my spiritual strength';[3] and a few lines later he adds: 'To be the cause of someone else's sufferings and joys, without possessing any positive right thereto — is that not the sweetest nourishment for our pride?'[4] In his diary entry for 12th June he even goes so far as to state: 'There are moments when I understand the vampire'.[5]

Nor are these merely theoretical pronouncements, for in practice Pechorin does indeed manipulate other people for his own pleasure. He enjoys teasing the hapless Grushnitsky, he kidnaps and seduces Bela, and he trifles with the naive young Princess Mary's affections, partly for want of anything else to occupy his time, and partly in order to spite Grushnitsky. Furthermore, Lermontov's hero is also implicated, directly or indirectly, in more than one death: he kills Grushnitsky in a duel, and he is a prime mover in the violent deaths of Bela and her father. By the time we read the last episode in the novel, *The Fatalist*, we have become so used to associating Pechorin with death that it is hard not to think that he must somehow also be the cause of Vulich's violent end — though of course he is not.

If Pechorin manifested only these obvious and undeniable vices, he could easily be dismissed as nothing more than a cold-hearted and ruthless aristocratic rake, but he does possess on the other hand a number of impressive virtues which should be emphasised, not just to produce a balanced picture of the man, but also — more interestingly — because they tend to be overlooked by many critics and readers of the novel.

Before examining Pechorin's virtues though, something should be said about the subject of fatalism, which arises at various points in *A Hero of Our Time*. After all, if the theory of fatalism were correct, then the words *vice* and *virtue* would have very little significance; if all our actions were controlled — perhaps even planned in advance — by fate or any other higher force, rather than freely chosen by ourselves, then we could not meaningfully be either rebuked for our apparently bad deeds, or praised for our apparently good ones; any vices or virtues would have to be ascribed to fate, rather than to individual men and women. Of course, as Lermontov well knew, in spite of his story *The Fatalist*, no conclusive experiments can be set up to test the theory of fatalism, and in practice, most of the time, we all take for granted that we do possess a considerable measure of freedom. Pechorin certainly assumes this much more often than not, and — for the duration of the present discussion at least — so must we.

What, then, are Pechorin's virtues? First of all, he possesses the traditional masculine virtues of physical toughness and energy, self-confidence and courage; he has a strong will and a commanding presence, and in dangerous situations he enjoys the advantages of quick reactions and a cool head. All these features emerge at their magnificent best in the duel with Grushnitsky — a scene which is one of the most memorable in all Russian literature.

Together with these masculine qualities, Pechorin also possesses what are often regarded as the more typically feminine virtues of personal charm (when he chooses to display it), good taste and a cultivated sense of elegance. He himself always dresses with great care, seeing himself as a consummate dandy even when galloping across the countryside in Circassian costume. At the same time he also appreciates elegance in others — from the impeccable *haute couture* of Princess Mary and her mother to the delicately-shaped nose of the smuggler-girl in *Taman'*. Lermontov's hero is exceptionally sensitive to the beauty of nature and has a highly developed sense of poetry — not so much the poetry of literature, as the poetry of life: one of the reasons he despises people like Grushnitsky is because, even though they may possess all sorts of good qualities, there is not, as he puts it, 'a penn'orth of poetry in their souls.'[6]

Beyond these two sets of attributes, which may be characterised as masculine and feminine, Pechorin possesses also the cerebral virtues of intelligence and wit, powers of logical analysis and, perhaps above all, intellectual honesty. He shows an uncanny ability to predict other people's reactions as well as a keen insight into his own complex personality, and one of his most constant and completely authentic preoccupations is his search for the truth — the truth about himself, society, human nature and the meaning of life. 'Why have I lived? For what purpose was I born?' he asks himself on the eve of the duel, not for the first, nor for the last time.[7]

With this range of characteristics Pechorin presents indeed an impressive and most unusual combination of thinker and man of action, and of poet and man of the world. Moreover, he is attractive — both to his fellow-characters in *A Hero of Our Time* and to countless readers of Lermontov's novel. Unlike so many other fictional heroes in Russian nineteenth-century literature, Pechorin at his best possesses a wonderful freshness and vitality, and is not the slightest bit bookish, or seedy, or pale. To employ a modern cult word, he is the least wet hero in all Russian literature.

Why, then, do all these good points in Pechorin tend, at worst to be almost completely overlooked, and at best to be dismissed as matters of little account in comparison with his failings?

First of all, if the novel is viewed from a modern English standpoint it is clear that many of Pechorin's positive qualities are unfashionable. Since the end of the Second World War English society has been, on the whole, more than usually suspicious of Pechorin's military, aristocratic and aesthetic virtues. (That is to say, Pechorin's determination and courage might be seen as military qualities; his self-confidence, proud individualism, and indeed generally effortless superiority number among the traditional marks of the ideal aristocrat; while his sensitivity, elegance, and good taste are aesthetic merits). In recent years English society has come close to ignoring these virtues and, rightly or wrongly, has placed instead a correspondingly higher value on qualities which Pechorin certainly does not possess, such as compassion, community-mindedness and a sense of fairness and social justice.

Secondly, if *A Hero of Our Time* is considered in its native context, it must be noted that Pechorin's virtues have rarely been widely fashionable in Russia, where traditions of energetic personal independence have never really taken root, and individual enterprise has seldom been generally applauded. Further — and this is perhaps a more important point for the present discussion — nor are Pechorin's virtues those traditionally associated with the main stream of Russian nineteenth- and twentieth-century literature. From about 1840 Russian literature became committed, by and large, to the ideals of social reform and humanitarian or religious progress; political and religious writers alike stressed man's duty to society and his fellows, and preached — or at least tacitly assumed — that self-sacrifice in the interest of others was by far the greatest of all virtues.

Indeed, much subsequent Russian nineteenth-century literature — certainly a good deal of Tolstoy and Dostoevsky — can be interpreted as an attempt to combat the self-assertive tendency expressed by Pechorin. In *Crime and Punishment*, for instance, Dostoevsky strongly rebuts Raskolnikov's Pechorin-like arguments about the morally privileged position of his class of superior men, while in *The Brothers Karamazov* all the self-assertive urges seething through the novel are countered by Father Zosima's doctrine of self-denial and universal love. So too in *War and Peace*: Tolstoy's heroes, Prince Andrew and Pierre, both come to accept the need to reject self-indulgence and worldly ostentation. Perhaps the most striking rejection of Pechorinism is to be found in Tolstoy's *Father Sergius*, which portrays a model hero achieving salvation by progressing from his position as the most brilliant figure at the court of Nicholas I to labouring in Siberia as an anonymous, humble monk.

Like Russian literature, Russian literary criticism too adopted from about 1840 a predominantly moralistic approach. Nineteenth-century Russian critics, like their Soviet successors today, tended to assess works of literature chiefly according to their social utility and were inclined to measure literary characters principally against an ethical yardstick. Clearly, Pechorin could not be awarded high marks by such examiners. It is interesting to note, though, that even Belinsky, when writing a long review of Lermontov's novel in 1840, was able to stress the power of both sides of Pechorin's nature: '...a certain greatness shines through his very vices, like lightning through black storm-clouds, and he is beautiful and full of poetry even at those moments when our human feeling rises against him...'.[8]

A third reason for overlooking Pechorin's virtues derives from Lermontov himself – or more precisely from the oft-quoted remark in his *Foreword* to the second edition of the novel: 'The Hero of Our Time, my dear sirs, is certainly a portrait, but not of a single person. It is a portrait composed of the vices of our entire generation in their ultimate development'.[9] Accepted at face value and taken in isolation from the novel itself, these words certainly pronounce a clear and forceful condemnation of Pechorin — but should the reader accept the statement so straightforwardly?

First of all it must be remembered that Lermontov is a writer who delights in ambiguity and irony and who indeed only a few lines earlier in the same *Foreword* has warned against a literal acceptance of all statements made in works of literature. Secondly — and more importantly — it is obvious that the attitude towards Pechorin expressed in this *Foreword* (written, it will be recalled, only for the second edition of *A Hero of Our Time* and in defence of the work) contrasts markedly with that found in the *Foreword to Pechorin's Diary* where the narrator praises Pechorin's sincerity and suggests that the reader's main effort should be directed towards understanding and exonerating him.[10]

Thirdly — and most important of all — it is hard to maintain that in the main body of the text attention focuses primarily on Pechorin's viciousness. Rather do we find that his virtues are given prominence and that he is indeed portrayed not only with sympathy but also with a marked degree of affection and admiration.

Some of Lermontov's contemporaries believed this to stem from the autobiographical nature of Pechorin. True, in his *Foreword* to the second edition of the novel Lermontov denies that Pechorin is a self-portrait, but both Turgenev and Belinsky were unconvinced, while Ivan Panaev, who frequently met Lermontov in St Petersburg in the 1830s, states quite plainly: 'There is no doubt that he depicted in Pechorin, if not himself, then at least an ideal which concerned him at that time and to which he strongly aspired.'[11]

Perhaps, then, Lermontov's remark about Pechorin's presenting a composite portrait of a whole generation's vices was not unreservedly true, but on this point, as on many others, every reader of *A Hero of Our Time* must make up his own mind. Whatever other responses he may provoke,

Pechorin certainly forces readers to think and to consider their own attitudes and values. In the last analysis perhaps that is his greatest virtue and the supreme vindication of Lermontov's novel.

NOTES

1. M. Yu. Lermontov, *Polnoe sobranie sochinenii v pyati tomakh,* Moscow-Leningrad, 1935-37, V, p.186.
2. *P.S.S.*, V, p.229.
3. *P.S.S.*, V, p.270. In the 1937 edition the date for this entry in Pechorin's diary is given as June 11th, not June 3rd. This apparent anomaly arises from the fact that Lermontov's original manuscript gave alternative dates for all entries after May 21st. The normal practice now is to use these alternative dates.
4. *P.S.S.*, V, p.271.
5. *P.S.S.*, V, p.286.
6. *P.S.S.*, V, p.242.
7. *P.S.S.*, V, p.296.
8. V.G. Belinskii, 'Geroi nashego vremeni. Sochinenie M. Lermontova' (*Polnoe sobranie sochinenii v trinadtsati tomakh,* Moscow, 1953-59, IV, p.236).
9. *P.S.S.*, V, p.186.
10. *P.S.S.*, V, p.229.
11. I.I. Panaev, 'Iz literaturnykh vospominanii', *M.Yu. Lermontov v vospominaniyakh sovremennikov,* Penza, 1960, p.179.

FURTHER READING ON LERMONTOV

Laurence Kelly: *Lermontov. Tragedy in the Caucasus*, Constable, London, 1977.
Janko Lavrin, *Lermontov*, Bowes & Bowes, London, 1959.
John Mersereau Jr, *Mikhail Lermontov*, Southern Illinois Press, Illinois, 1962.

N.V. Gogol 1809-52

III

GOGOL: THE GREATCOAT

The Greatcoat is the story of an impoverished civil service clerk, in St Petersburg, who by dint of great sacrifices manages to buy himself a new coat, but is robbed of it the very first evening he wears it. He tries to get it back by going to see a highly-placed official who gives him such a reprimand that the poor clerk falls ill and dies. Later his ghost haunts St Petersburg, stealing coats; it is only laid to rest when it has taken the greatcoat of the highly-placed official himself.

The story is often regarded as having initiated a whole tradition of Russian realism. 'We have all come out of Gogol's greatcoat' is a remark allegedly uttered by Dostoevsky (though this attribution is suspect). Yet in what sense can a story with a ghost sequence be called realistic? By realism Russian critics in the nineteenth century often meant 'critical realism', implying that a writer by portraying society 'realistically' was thereby expressing criticism of it. On the face of it the plot of *The Greatcoat*, as outlined, does suggest a social theme and it cannot be denied that criticism is implicit in Gogol's treatment of the police (in particular his laughter at the inept constables). Veneration of rank and the insolence of authority (the 'Important Person') are presented with implied censure. Yet, as regards his poverty, the authorities in Akakii Akakievich's own department are not responsible for his plight. The director gives him a much higher bonus than he had expected when he needs the money for his coat. Afterwards the assistant chief clerk invites him to a party, partly in honour of his coat. Nor can it be argued that the civil service has turned Akakii Akakievich into the automaton that he undoubtedly is. Indeed, he seems to have been born to his role and we learn that he had once been given more interesting work but had proved incapable of it.

Nor is it entirely true that he is portrayed sympathetically. If the other clerks poke fun at him, they do little more than the narrator of the story himself; for in spite of his strictures on those writers who mock titular councillors, he nevertheless constantly presents his own hero as a figure of fun, with a neck that reminds him of a toy plaster-kitten, and the strange ability always to find himself under a window when rubbish is being thrown out.

Moreover the poverty of Akakii Akakievich, which is the corner-stone for any social interpretation of the work, cannot be taken at its face value; it is always presented with hyperbole. In the first place, Akakii Akakievich is by no means at the bottom of the hierarchy of ranks — he is in the ninth grade, which means there were another five grades below his. Other titular councillors in Gogol do not appear to be in such financial straits. Poprishchin, for instance, in *The Diary of a Madman* goes to the theatre, reads the journal *The Northern Bee* and orders a new uniform. Nor in *The Greatcoat* itself is poverty stressed in the lives of the other minor civil servants, whose leisure time is full of theatre-going, card-playing and tea-drinking. Indeed, all their various activities are used as a contrast to set off the absolute lack of any outside activity on the part of Akakii Akakievich himself.

A contrast can also be seen in the figure of the assistant chief clerk who, if Akakii Akakievich seems incredibly poor, appears on the other hand to be exaggeratedly affluent. He is, after all, only the assistant chief clerk, yet he not only lives in the better part of St Petersburg, but occupies the best part of the house — the first floor. He has servants, is able to throw a lavish party without any difficulty and invites guests whose coats have beaver-fur collars and velvet lapels.

Akakii Akakievich has absolutely no social life and no dependents, is over fifty and has been in the department for longer than anyone can remember, yet he is apparently unable to afford something as essential as a proper coat to keep out the St Petersburg frost. It is not as though he is incompetent in monetary affairs. For every rouble which he spends he always puts half a copeck away in a money box. By this means he has already accumulated half the sum necessary for his new coat — forty roubles. According to Akakii Akakievich's system of saving, this must represent a total of eight thousand roubles which he has spent 'in the course of several years', so that, as he receives four hundred roubles per year, it represents twenty years' salary. (The actual period of saving might not be as long as this, since we know that he gets bonuses from the director.)

He is expecting a bonus for the holiday, but it is allotted in advance for other clothing:

> It was necessary to get some new trousers, to pay the bootmaker an old debt for vamping old boot-tops, and he also had to order three shirts from the seamstress, and a couple of items of that underwear which it is unseemly to mention by name in print.[1]

The coyness of the comic tone suggests that this is not to be taken at its face value, and indeed after his death none of this other clothing is mentioned:

> They did not seal his room, nor any of his things, because in the first place there were no heirs, and in the second place, very little inheritance had been left, to be precise — a bunch of goose quills, a

quire of white official paper, three pairs of socks, two or three buttons which had dropped off his trousers, and the dressing-gown, already well known to the reader.[2]

Yet the boots and the underclothing had earlier figured prominently in his budget, for he had resolved:

> when walking along the streets, to step on the stones and paving as lightly and carefully as possible, almost on tiptoe, so that by these means he would not wear out his soles quickly; to give his undergarments to be washed by the laundress as seldom as possible; and in order to prevent them getting too dirty from wear, to take them off every time he came home, and wear only a fustian dressing-gown, which was very ancient and had been spared even by time itself.[3]

All this is grotesque: the poverty of Akakii Akakievich is not credible in real terms. If all the titular councillors of Tsar Nicholas I were as inexplicably indigent, he would never have had a civil service. Yet although the material poverty of Akakii Akakievich is open to question, what is not in doubt is his spiritual poverty: it is not Akakii Akakievich's lack of material resources which is striking, but the paucity of his spiritual resources. Gogol is here employing a device central to his portrayal of psychological states: the external world reflects an inner world and in Akakii Akakievich's outward indigence we have a metaphor of his inner poverty.

Akakii Akakievich's inner world is completely obsessive. He has only one passion — the copying out of words:

> One could scarcely find a man who lived so much in his job. It is not enough to say that he worked with zeal, no, he worked with love. In his copying he was aware of a world of his own which was pleasant and full of variety.[4]

His love of writing is not merely a job; his leisure hours, spent at home, are devoted to his one great passion. Even when walking about the streets he is incapable of thinking about anything else:

> But if Akakii Akakievich looked at anything, then everywhere he saw his own clear lines, written in an even hand, and only if a horse's muzzle sprang out of nowhere, lodged itself on his shoulder and blew out through its nostrils a whole wind on to his cheek, only then would he notice that he was not in the middle of a line, but rather in the middle of the street.[5]

This day-dream quality associated with Akakii Akakievich's copying is suggestive of 'writing' of a different order. Our hero might almost be a writer in a more fundamental sense — a man obsessed by words like Gogol himself. But Akakii Akakievich's imagination is caught not by the content and significance of words, but by their outward form; their most palpable material expression. Even in his inner world surface has ousted content.

Akakii Akakievich's obsession with words is understandable: communication is his central problem. When he is given a job which entails the alteration and the *use* of words rather than merely *copying* them, he is at a complete loss. In daily life too, communication is difficult because of his lack of words:

> It must be explained that Akakii Akakievich expressed himself for the most part in prepositions, adverbs, and ultimately in particles which had absolutely no meaning whatever. If, indeed, it were a very difficult matter, he even had the habit of leaving his phrases unfinished, so that very frequently he would begin his utterance with the words: 'It, indeed, is absolutely, and that,' and then there was just nothing else at all, and he himself would have forgotten, believing that he had already said everything.[6]

Akakii Akakievich not only lacks words himself, he is at the mercy of the words of others, even of the rhetorical effects of Petrovich, the one-eyed tailor, who, we are told:

> ...was very fond of powerful effects. He liked in some way or other suddenly to take people completely aback and then look sideways to see what sort of face the bewildered person would pull at such words.[7]

The 'powerful effect' of Petrovich, the price he quotes for a new coat, is the device of hyperbole. It challenges the indigence of Akakii Akakievich on both its levels: the material and the verbal.

In all Akakii Akakievich's obsessive copying of words, what he seeks to make his own is not *beauty of style* but *communication* with someone unknown or someone important:

> ...he would purposely take a copy for himself, for his own pleasure, particularly if the document was distinguished, not by the beauty of its style, but by the fact that it was addressed to some new or important person.[8]

When, however, in real life he tries to communicate with a 'new and important person' (the general to whom he is advised to turn for help), he is a second time devastated by words:

> But the important person, pleased by the fact that the effect had even surpassed all expectations and completely intoxicated by the thought that a word from him could even deprive a man of his senses, glanced sideways at his friend to find out how he looked on the matter.[9]

Here the interview with the general seems consciously to be likened to the earlier visit to the tailor: both love *effekty*, and both look sideways to see what reaction there is to their words. The interview with Petrovich ends: '...and Akakii Akakievich went out, completely annihilated after such words'. With the general, however, the 'annihilation' is no longer metaphorical: after his words Akakii Akakievich takes to his bed and dies.

Akakii Akakievich's obsession with the outer form of words, with their well-executed graphic clothing, is a mark of his desire to be master of them, and at the same time it is a sad comment on his inability to capture their content. He is thus a character in a well-known Gogolian mould, caught between the 'visible laughter' of the outer surface and the 'unseen tears' of the inner world. Yet there is one person with whom he does appear to be able to communicate. On collecting his wits in the street after his first visit to Petrovich, we are told that he:

> ...began to converse with himself, not jerkily any more, but reasonably and frankly, as though with a sensible friend, with whom one could have a chat about something intimate and near to one's heart.[10]

Communication which is difficult with others seems easy with himself — the one friend he has. Nevertheless there is another 'friend' who comes into his life, a friend who significantly has his own outward form — his new greatcoat. He must endure privations if he is to gain it. He must go without food. Eating for him previously had been the act of an insentient creature (he only realised that it was time to stop when he saw that his stomach had swollen) but now the idea of the coat represents a new 'spiritual' sustenance:

> He even trained himself to go without food in the evenings, but on the other hand he had spiritual food, for he bore in his thoughts the eternal idea of the future coat. From that time on it was as though his very existence had become somehow fuller, as though he had got married, as though some other person were present alongside him, as though he were not alone, as though some congenial life-long lady-friend had agreed to go together with him along life's way – and this lady-friend was none other than that very overcoat with its thick padding and strong lining that would not wear out.[11]

The 'eternal titular councillor' has found his mate not in the 'external feminine' but in the 'eternal idea' of his new coat. A man without content has fallen in love with his new facade. The effect the coat has on his personality is remarkable:

> He became somehow livelier, even firmer in character, like a man who
> had determined and set himself a goal. Doubt and indecision, in a
> word all wavering and vague traits, disappeared of their own accord
> from his face and his behaviour. From time to time fire showed in his
> eyes, and the most daring and bold thoughts flashed through his
> mind: 'Should I not really put marten on the collar?'[12]

The entertaining of 'the most daring and bold thoughts' in respect of the
coat seems to be carrying on the sexual motif, and certainly the coat has
replaced his old love: 'Once, when copying a document, he nearly even
made a mistake, so that he exclaimed 'ugh!' almost audibly and crossed
himself.'[13]

When he has enough money to buy the material for his coat, 'his heart
usually quite quiet, began to beat'; and the day on which the coat was
actually brought to him is given almost ceremonial importance by one of
the narrator's verbal formulae:

> It was...it is difficult to say on what precise day, but probably on the
> most solemn of days in Akakii Akakievich's life, that Petrovich finally
> brought the coat.[14]

This most solemn of days in the life of Akakii Akakievich might almost be
a wedding. Certainly the festive occasion is linked to an awakening of
feeling: 'In the meantime, Akakii Akakievich went along in the most
festive disposition of all his feelings',[15] and this new outward form has
even brought him 'inner happiness'.

This sense of a special occasion is carried on in the treatment Akakii
Akakievich receives at the office. It is suggested that he should throw a
party that evening so that his colleagues can drink to the coat. Akakii
Akakievich is saved from further embarrassment only by the intervention
of the assistant chief clerk who invites everybody round to his apartment
instead, as it so happens that it is his name-day:

> The whole of that day was for Akakii Akakievich just like the greatest
> solemn festival. He returned home in the happiest frame of mind.

His whole way of life appears to be changing:

> He dined cheerfully and after dinner he did not write anything, not a
> single document, but just lay like a sybarite on the bed, until it got
> dark.[16]

He then puts on his greatcoat and sets out for the party.

The section which follows is one of the key sections of the story. The
narrator loses his memory when he wishes to give the precise location in St
Petersburg of the apartment of the assistant chief clerk. (It does not matter

that he has not bothered to tell us where Akakii Akakievich lives, nor where he works.) The problem of where the assistant chief clerk lives, however, is solved by one of the narrator's verbal formulae:

> What is at least certain is that the civil servant lived in the better part of the town, therefore not at all near to Akakii Akakievich.[17]

The formula seeks to emphasise the social distance between two worlds, but the distance is also psychological. The physical landmarks of the route, as the narrator confesses by way of excuse, are all confused in his head:

> ...and everything that there is in St Petersburg, all the streets and the houses have become so fused and jumbled in one's head that it is difficult to get anything out of there in a decent form.[18]

Certainly, there seems to be a parallel between what is going on in the streets of St Petersburg and what is going on in another head — that of Akakii Akakievich. His movement into greater life is not merely a physical progression, but reflects a process going on within Akakii Akakievich himself. Once more we have an example of Gogol's central device; the outer world is a metaphor for the inner:

> At first Akakii Akakievich had to pass through several desolate streets with feeble lighting, but the more he drew near to the apartment of the civil servant, the livelier the streets became, the more populated and the more powerfully illuminated.[19]

His progress is from desolation to life — from darkness to light, and now the former automaton, who never used to notice anything in the street, seems to have his eyes open for the first time: 'He looked at all this as though it were something new.'

An even more amazing awakening seems to be taking place:

> He stopped with curiosity before the lighted window of a shop to look at a picture which depicted a beautiful woman, who was throwing off her shoe, and thus exposing her whole leg, and not a bad one at that, while behind her back a man with side whiskers and a beautiful goatee beard below his lip had stuck his head through the doorway from another room. Akakii Akakievich shook his head from side to side, grinned, and then went on his way. Why did he grin? Was it because he had encountered a thing that was completely unknown to him, but about which each one of us has retained some sort of sixth sense, or like many other civil servants, did he think the following: 'Well, those French! If they take a fancy to something like that, then it is, indeed, just as it were...'? But perhaps he did not even think that – it is after all impossible to get inside the soul of another man and find out everything that he thinks.[20]

Thus the narrator disclaims all attempt at psychological analysis. Yet his own speculations, before his assertion that it is impossible to get inside another man, not only call attention to Akakii Akakievich's state of mind, they suggest his ambiguity of response in an evocative way. A similarly effective denial of psychological insight occurs after the loss of the coat when Akakii Akakievich has returned home and gone to bed:

> ...and how he spent the night there may be judged by those who are capable to any extent of imagining the situation of another man.[21]

Gogol, in rejecting any possibility of getting inside his characters, is not abandoning the attempt to portray their psychology. He merely proceeds by different means. Akakii Akakievich wears his new greatcoat like a different frame of mind; his brand-new outward form is his new self. At the same time the greatcoat also has for him associations of a new relationship, a 'life-long lady-friend', so that when in his progress through the 'streets' of St Petersburg, he encounters sexual titillation, perhaps for the first time, his reactions are ambiguous — but not as ambiguous as the narrator would have us believe.

———————————

The opening paragraph of *The Greatcoat* should be a warning to the reader. It is long, involved and absolutely irrelevant to the story itself. In fact the opening paragraph is a sort of verbal arabesque which goes nowhere, except back to its original starting point: from 'In one of our government departments' to '...a certain department.'

It is typical of Gogol to take his reader on a long aside which will go nowhere. As a form of humour it may be compared to the shaggy dog story, where the joke is not *for* the listener but *on* the listener. It is, of course, a dangerous game to play with a reader, who can always terminate the joke by putting the book down. Moreover, such a joke implies a latent hostility towards the reader. Yet if the anecdote in the opening paragraph about the police inspector has any point at all, it is to suggest quite the reverse, namely that readers (especially those in official positions) are only too prone to show hostility towards authors.

The narrator of the story is, of course, not Gogol himself. It is someone who is very naive, not at all well educated, and who as a teller of a story is incredibly inept. He repeatedly concentrates on inessential and often absurd details, at the expense of the plot itself — and in this sense the opening paragraph is a foretaste of what is to come. (The inept narrator is a favourite device with Gogol, and this type of tale — a story told by an illiterate narrator — is quite common in Russian literature).

But although the narrator is naive, the narrative, in effect, is not: it is full of hints, innuendoes, puns and verbal tricks of all sorts. It is through these that the tale really unfolds, and in a way which gives hidden depth to a seemingly shallow surface.

One of the great ironies of this style is that the naive narrator requires a sophisticated reader, a reader who is sensitive, not to the possibilities of personal libel, as those whom Gogol mocks in the opening paragraph, but one who is sensitive to words and tone and word-play.

Naive ambiguity is a constant feature of the narrative technique in *The Greatcoat*. There are many puns which communicate a waywardness and playfulness of tone to the narrative, yet their contribution is not so much to the humour of the story as to the external presentation of the inner world of the central character, a man who is himself obsessed by the outward form of words, their graphic contours, only because their real content and function eludes him. The pun is precisely this: a word taken at face value which nevertheless has a hidden content beneath its deceptive surface. The verbal play has more meaning than is at first apparent, and the relationship between facade and interior is not only the central 'device' of *The Greatcoat*, it is the architectural principle which informs its shape.

There is a great deal of verbal play at the opening of the story, (i.e. the whole of the introductory section ending with the play on the word 'councillor'). In introducing Akakii Akakievich the narrator places exaggerated importance on the naming of his hero, whereas his formative years are merely bridged by a verbal formula: 'The child was christened. At which he began to cry and he pulled such a face as though he sensed beforehand that he would be a titular councillor.'[22] Almost immediately after this we find him already long established in the office as a copy clerk: '...so that later people became convinced that he had obviously been born into the world ready-made, in a uniform and a bald patch on his head'. [23] His christening seems to pre-ordain his profession and his profession seems to have been entered on at birth.

This emphasis on his christening and lack of interest in his formative years suggests that his name is far more important than his life in determining his character. In particular the origin of the surname is treated with naive seriousness:

> The civil servant's name was Bashmachkin. From the very name itself one can see that at some time it had been derived from a shoe; but when, at what particular time and in what way it was derived from a shoe – nothing of this is known. Both his father and his grandfather, and even his brother-in-law, all Bashmachkins through and through, used to walk about in boots, changing the soles only three times a year.[24]

The whole of this explanation is patently absurd, if taken at its surface meaning. Yet, on another level, it suggests a whole train of semantic ambiguities which are picked up and developed later in the story, and in such a way as to reveal the psychological problems of Akakii Akakievich himself.

In the first place the verb 'derived' is taken quite literally, (the all important qualification 'word' which ought to precede 'shoe' is omitted) so that our hero's name appears to have come directly from an article of footwear — a shoe (just as later it will be suggested that he has almost got married to a greatcoat). Through his surname the hero is thus directly identified with a mere casing of the human body.

The narrator compounds the absurdity by asserting that all Akakii Akakievich's family wore boots, and gives the irrelevant information that they had the soles replaced only three times a year. (The saving of his soles will later figure prominently in Akakii Akakievich's economies needed to acquire the coat.) The list of Akakii Akakievich's relatives, who, according to the narrator, are all genuine Bashmachkins includes 'even a brother-in-law' (*i dazhe shurin*) despite the fact that, as this is a relationship by marriage, he could not possibly be a genuine Bashmachkin as the narrator claims. Yet the inclusion of this brother-in-law is absurd in an even more profound sense. Russian relationships by marriage are very precise, and *shurin* can only mean 'wife's brother'. For Akakii Akakievich to have a '*shurin*', he must also have a wife, but a wife is no more in evidence than these other relatives with whom he is here credited. Akakii Akakievich is completely alone. This little verbal puzzle, therefore, tangles the 'shoe' from which his name is derived, with the relatives from whom he is actually derived (his father and his grandfather) and ties them in with a figure to whom he can only be related by a sexual bond (the brother-in-law).

The theme of the wife, who is non-existent but implied, appears again when the narrator gives examples of his 'down-trodden' existence, such as the teasing to which he is subjected at the office:

> They would relate, right in front of him, various stories concocted about him. They said about his landlady, an old woman of seventy, that she beat him, and they would ask him when their wedding would be. They would scatter paper on his head, calling it snow.[25]

The motif of the 'shoe' is prominent in the picture which stirs a vague sexual awakening in Akakii Akakievich, and the detail seems intentional, for virtually the same picture is described at the end of *The Nose*, but without the mention of a shoe. At a later stage a shoe will also link this picture with his landlady. Thus the 'shoe', from which his outward identification (his name) is derived, suggests a latent sexual motif in much the same way as does that other item of apparel, his other outward form, the greatcoat.

Akakii Akakievich's progress through St Petersburg may be interpreted as a journey in self-exploration: it is certainly a progress towards light. He moves away from his own badly-lit part of the city, past the lighted window with its erotic picture to the apartment of the civil servant who has invited him; 'the assistant chief clerk lived in great style; there was a lantern shining on the staircase'.[26]

The fact that Akakii Akakievich is at first overawed is again suggested by Gogol's external method of psychological portrayal. Akakii Akakievich is reduced to the status of an object among other objects:

> On entering the hall Akakii Akakievich saw on the floor a whole row of galoshes. Among them in the middle of the room stood a samovar, noisily emitting clouds of steam. On the walls hung nothing but greatcoats and capes, among which there were several which even had beaver collars or velvet lapels.[27]

It seems significant that he is confronted with footwear and greatcoats. The only thing which appears to have life in this ante-room is another inanimate object — the samovar. Real life once more, it seems, is going on elsewhere: for on the other side of the wall he can hear the noise of the party. The guests have already been assembled for some time.

Nevertheless the occasion has been held partly to honour Akakii Akakievich's new coat. He is accepted by this society, and his greatcoat is rapturously admired, even though there are better ones hanging up in the hall. 'Then, of course, everybody dropped him and his coat and turned, as is the custom, to the whist-tables.'[28] After all, Akakii Akakievich is not really at home in these surroundings. He tries to creep away, but is made to stay for supper and two festive glasses of champagne. It is after midnight when he escapes. He finds his coat, 'which, not without regret, he perceived was lying on the floor'.[29] He carefully shakes it, and goes down to a still lighted street. Here, sexual promptings (inexplicable to the narrator) once more well up within him:

> Akakii Akakievich went along in a gay mood, and for some unknown reason he was even almost on the point of running up behind some lady or other, who went past like lightning, and every part of whose body was full of unusual movement. However, he stopped at once and went on as before very slowly, amazed himself at this unaccountable burst of speed.[30]

His progress now, however, is away from light and conviviality towards the dark, shuttered emptiness of his own quarter of the town.

On his outward journey he had been *looking* for the first time in his life. Now, as he crosses a dark square, where a light seems 'at the world's end' and 'it is as though there is a sea around him', our explorer closes his eyes — and is robbed of his greatcoat by men with moustaches. Thus he is brutally deprived of the promise of that fuller life which had been offered to him so briefly and so tenuously.

He goes home to his landlady and the details of his return seem to reproduce in ironical terms the elements of the picture in the lighted window which had earlier aroused such strange stirrings within him:

> The old lady, the landlady of his apartment, hearing the terrible knocking at the door, hurriedly jumped out of bed and with a shoe on only one foot, ran to open the door, holding her nightshirt to her bosom out of modesty.[31]

The landlady, as we know, has already been associated with the marital status of Akakii Akakievich by the clerks at the office, who teased him about marrying her and scattered 'snow' on his head. Now, when he comes back covered in real snow, his landlady, like the woman in the picture, confronts him with 'a shoe on one foot' and a hint of sexual titillation ('holding her nightshirt to her bosom, out of modesty'). But the 'man at the door' is not the dandy with the side whiskers and beautiful beard; it is the dishevelled Akakii Akakievich, with what little hair he has in complete disarray.

So Akakii Akakievich is thrown back on his seventy-year-old landlady, by the 'light' of whose candle he used to work in the evenings (after first having taken off his underwear to economise on laundry!). On her advice he goes to the police, but the district superintendent seems to think that the loss of the coat is in some way connected with its owner's dissolute life:

> The district superintendent received the story of the theft of the coat somehow in an exceedingly strange way. Instead of turning his attention to the main point of the matter, he began to question Akakii Akakievich as to why he was returning home so late, and hadn't he called in at some disorderly house or other?[32]

Here, as elsewhere in the story, the significance of the coat is interpreted not in terms of the obvious, but in terms of a suggested sexual theme. The hint is present even on his death-bed, for he keeps asking his landlady to drag a coat-thief out from under his blankets.

If in the opening section of *The Greatcoat* verbal play is an important device for establishing motifs which are to be developed in the central section of the story, now in the final section (the ghost sequence) verbal play has a similar function. There is a recurring pun on the concepts of 'dead' and 'alive'. The police are ordered to apprehend the '*dead man* dead or alive'. One of them apparently succeeds, but loses the ghost because he pauses to take snuff of a quality 'which even a dead man couldn't stand', and from that time on the police 'got so frightened of dead men, that they were even fearful of arresting the living'. Finally, there is an 'apparition' at the end of the story, who when challenged by a policeman, shows him a huge fist 'such as you would not find on the living'.

All this seems like humour directed at the police, who throughout the story have shown themselves to be particularly inept, but there is also a serious intention behind the word-play. The ghost is first introduced as 'a dead man in the form of a civil servant' (*mertvets v vide chinovnika*). Later he is simply referred to as the 'dead man-civil servant' (*chinovnik-mertvets*). The verbal play on 'dead' and 'alive' is therefore a motif pointing to the artistic function of the story's fantastic ending; it raises the whole question of '*chinovnik-mertvets*'.

When he was alive, Akakii Akakievich was in reality more like a 'civil servant in the form of a dead man'. The promise of an awakening into life, flimsy though it may have been, was cruelly taken from him by men with moustaches. When he has died he returns as a 'dead man in the form of a civil servant' to avenge himself and, by one of those ironies in which the story abounds, he proves to be more effective as a dead man, than he was when alive.

It is typical of Gogol that this inversion to which the central character is subjected should also be reflected in the external world around him. When earlier Akakii Akakievich was going through the streets of St Petersburg, the narrator was insistent that everything in the city was so muddled in his head that he could not remember names; now, when his hero appears as a ghost, he is very meticulous about giving the precise location of each appearance. In the first instance a real man was going through a spiritual city; in the second a spirit man is haunting a concrete and actual city.

It is only after the ghost has robbed the 'important person' of his greatcoat that this unquiet spirit is finally laid, and the whole incident is presented with the same ironic parallelism of detail which has been noted elsewhere in the story. The important person, having just learned of the death of Akakii Akakievich, goes to a party to cheer himself up. (Akakii Akakievich had been to a party before he lost his coat.) Here (like Akakii Akakievich before him) he has two glasses of champagne. He feels in a gayer mood, and just as Akakii Akakievich had then, for some unknown reason, wanted to chase after a woman in the street, so the important person now entertains thoughts of an amorous nature:

> The champagne put him in a mood for special measures; that is he decided not to go home yet, but to call on a certain lady of his acquaintance, Karolina Ivanovna, a lady who appeared to be of German extraction, and for whom he felt an entirely friendly relationship.[33]

Here, as in the earlier incident with Akakii Akakievich, the narrator shows himself to be naively uncomprehending about the sexual motivation of his characters.

Whereas Akakii Akakievich had been making the first tentative gestures in the direction of life, the important person has long had it firmly in his

The Voice of a Giant

grasp. He takes an active part in the evening gathering as a man among equals; on leaving the party he is going to a real mistress; and moreover, unlike Akakii Akakievich, he also has a family:

> But the important person, although he was quite content with the family affection he received at home, considered it fitting to have a lady-friend in another part of town for friendly relationships. This lady-friend was not a whit better or younger than his wife. But such puzzles do exist in the world, and it is not for us to judge them.[34]

It seems poetic justice that the ghost should rob this 'man of substance' of his greatcoat at this precise moment. The effect is cathartic: the ghost is laid, and the general himself becomes a much better person.

The story ends with yet another ironic twist. Another ghost is seen and it is believed to be the ghost of Akakii Akakievich, but it is really an 'apparition' and when challenged by a particularly inept policeman it threatens him with a fist not unlike that of the man who had stolen Akakii Akakievich's greatcoat in the first place and had showed him a fist 'the size of a civil servant's head'. The policeman leaves the apparition alone:

> The apparition was, however, much taller and wore really enormous moustaches, and turning its steps, as it seemed, towards the Obukhov Bridge, it completely disappeared in the darkness of the night.[35]

Even Akakii Akakievich's credibility as a ghost, it seems, is being challenged by those men with moustaches and the whole story ends on a note of darkness.

NOTES

1. N.V. Gogol', *Polnoe sobranie sochinenii*, vv. I-XI, Moscow-Leningrad, 1937-1952, III, p.153. All subsequent references are given as page numbers in this volume.

2. p.168.	3. p.154.	4. p.144.	5. p.145.
6. p.449.	7. p.151.	8. pp.145-146.	9. p.167.
10. p.152.	11. p.154.	12. pp.154-155.	13. p.155.
14. p.156.	15. p.157.	16. p.158.	17. p.158.
18. p.158.	19. p.158.	20. pp.158-159.	21. p.162.
22. p.142.	23. p.143.	24. p.142.	25. p.143.
26. p.159.	27. p.159.	28. p.160.	29. p.160.
30. pp.160-161.	31. p.162.	32. p.163.	33. p.171.
34. p.172.	35. p.174.		

FURTHER READING ON GOGOL

Victor Erlich, *Gogol*, Yale University Press, Yale, 1969.
Vladimir Nabokov, *Nikolay Gogol*, Weidenfeld & Nicolson, London, 1973.
Richard Peace, *The Enigma of Gogol*, Cambridge University Press, Cambridge, 1981.

IV

TURGENEV: FATHERS AND SONS

The world-famous triumvirate which dominated nineteenth-century Russian realist prose consisted of three sharply differentiated writers: Turgenev, Dostoevsky and Tolstoy. Turgenev came first chronologically and was the first to become known abroad, though he has by now, according to general opinion, settled into third position on literary merit, with the other two competing for the accolade of supreme master. It is clear that Turgenev was incapable of Dostoevsky's profound and uncanny penetration into the workings of the human mind, or his expression of man's striving towards God. He lacks also Dostoevsky's exciting dynamism. Tolstoy, too, clearly outreaches Turgenev in the vastness and passion of his imagination and intellect alike.

Although Turgenev cannot approach the other two in breadth or depth of significance, he was nevertheless revered in his day by many of Europe and America's leading literary figures. Gustave Flaubert was among his most ardent admirers, and Henry James, who never faltered in his idolisation of Turgenev, imitated him in several of his own works — indeed, throughout half of his career. Ernest Hemingway advised aspiring writers to read everything Turgenev wrote, but for an extreme example of true devotion to Turgenev one can do no better than listen to the English critic and novelist Ford Madox Ford who once said: 'Shakespeare, if he had taken time to think upon these matters, would have been as great an artist as Turgenev.'[1] What are the qualities which created this grand reputation and ensured its survival?

In the first place, Turgenev is winsome rather than overwhelming. Nowhere in his work is the reader harangued by a demented Underground Man; nor will he be bored by idiosyncratic theorising on human history or distracted by rambling excursions intended to determine man's capacity for self-improvement. The only Turgenev who is allowed to intrude noticeably into his work is neither an analyst nor a preacher, but simply a genial narrator whose single concern is to persuade his reader to begin and sustain the agreeable suspension of disbelief upon which all fictional stories depend. The very mass of Turgenev's work is unformidable. His six novels taken together — *Rudin* (1856), *A Nest of Gentlefolk* (1859), *On the Eve* (1860), *Fathers and Sons* (1862), *Smoke* (1867) and *Virgin Soil* (1877) — are shorter than *War and Peace*. They come to about the length of *The Brothers Karamazov*. Turgenev is altogether easier to approach, to live with, to absorb and to understand.

I.S. Turgenev 1818-83

Another difference between Turgenev and his two great contemporaries is indicated in the way by which they became writers of prose. Whereas Tolstoy and Dostoevsky wrote important prose-works in their early or mid-twenties and never considered even the possibility of expressing themselves in poetry, Turgenev served a protracted and uncertain literary apprenticeship, wavering between poetry, sketches and drama before producing a real novel — and then only a short one — at the age of thirty-eight. The marks left upon him by his earlier careers as a poet, dramatist and writer of rural notes remained indelible and affected his finest mature work. Among other things, they led him to a love of language, a devotion to literary form, a neatness of construction, a hatred of all forms of extremism, a concern for beauty, and a gentleness of manner upon which his achievement as a writer and his whole reputation was founded. Most of these qualities work together and tend towards the principle of a peaceful and civilised enjoyment of life, with moderation in all things, including the settling of human differences, and a highly developed range of aesthetic sensibility. Alphonse Daudet summed up Turgenev as 'a feminine soul in the carcass of a cyclops.'[2] No aspersions on his masculinity are cast by this correct assessment of his literary qualities as being predominantly feminine. This applies to all of Turgenev, his matter and his manner. Whereas Dostoevsky deals with murderers and madmen, and Tolstoy describes warfare and destructive passions, Turgenev restricts himself for the most part — and certainly in the best of his tales and novels — to love stories. Moreover, they are not intrinsically compelling love stories. They lack sexuality and almost always end in some kind of failure, in almost Chekhovian non-events. They lack the ingredients which our twentieth century has come to look upon as the *sine qua non* of good literature — conflict, resolution, excitement and profound significance.

There are two ways, however, in which Turgenev indisputably excels and still claims a high position in the tradition of Russian realism: he fears comparison with no-one in his evocation of atmosphere or in his creation of authentic characters. Character is always at the centre of his claim to fame. This was where he always began his novels — with a single character, usually a real person or an amalgam of several real people. The one central figure would throw out spores which were to germinate into new characters. Turgenev would then take delight in working out complete dossiers on all of them, calculating the chronology of events with care, safeguarding consistency and meticulously interrelating them all. Many of these dossiers would later be transcribed verbatim into the resulting novel, in an unashamedly open digression which served a double purpose. It would delay the action of the story, thus creating a mild form of suspense and curiosity — the only sort this author was capable of — and it would envelop the character in a thick, warm cocoon of authenticity.

This is one reason why Turgenev is held to be a good example of the school of Realism: his fictional characters are shown against a perspective of rich biographical detail. Despite the scrupulous care exercised by Turgenev, he still made the occasional mistake in detail. One example concerns the age of Odintsova's sister, Katya, in *Fathers and Sons*. In Chapter XV we are told that she was only eight years younger than her sister when their father died, but the novel takes place when Anna is twenty-nine and Katya eighteen — the difference in their ages having expanded to eleven years. This kind of slip is, however, as rare as it is insignificant. The device itself enjoys repeated success in Turgenev's hands. His pen-portraits of Pavel Petrovich and Fenichka in *Fathers and Sons* are typical examples, the former taking up the whole of Chapter VII — it is quite common for such biographical digressions to occupy precisely one chapter — the latter involving only a portion of Chapter VIII. These vignettes, and dozens like them elsewhere in Turgenev's work, are drawn with compassion, consistency and a deep insight into human character. The device is unsubtle and yet honest. Turgenev simply says: 'And Arkadii told Bazarov his uncle's story. The reader will find it set out in the next chapter.'[3] (VI) This is a warm invitation to share the literary illusion with a genial narrator for mutual pleasure. The one notorious misuse of the flashback biography is in *A Nest of Gentlefolk*, where Fyodor Lavretsky's personal history is retraced to Vasilii the Blind in the fifteenth century and takes no less than ten chapters to work itself out. In that novel Turgenev brings the reader back to the present with an apologetic appeal to his good nature: '...we now ask the indulgent reader to return with us'.[4] This indicates the risk run by the device: a delay in the interests of suspense, authentication or curiosity may test the reader's patience, and large amounts of biographical detail, taken at a draught, may give rise to tedium. But the risk is almost always avoided by Turgenev, who scores success after success in these self-contained character-sketches.

An extension of this practice, incidentally, is to be seen in Turgenev's penchant for ending his stories with an epilogue. Each one of his six novels contains a tail-piece in which the narrator winds up the story and tells what happened subsequently to all the main characters, and often the minor ones too. Here is a prolongation of the illusion that we are looking at real people. We have watched them in action and interaction, learned about their past lives, and now we even follow them into their future, sometimes years after the novel has ended. *Rudin* and *A Nest of Gentlefolk* both end with an epilogue named as such, and also a detached terminal paragraph which serves almost as an epilogue to the epilogue. The last four novels have no chapter entitled 'Epilogue', but each uses its last chapter for the necessary and usual rounding-off purposes.

A similar concern for the appearance of actuality determines also the beginnings of Turgenev's novels. They open with a statement of the year and usually the season and the time of day. Only *Rudin* omits the actual year, beginning: 'It was a quiet summer morning'. We are told in the opening lines of all the others that they begin, respectively: 'In Spring 1842' (*A Nest of Gentlefolk*); '...in high summer 1853' (*On the Eve*); 'On May 20th 1859' (*Fathers and Sons*); 'On August 10th 1862' (*Smoke*); and 'In Spring 1868' (*Virgin Soil*). Only certain places are left indeterminate. It is seen as proper to name capital cities and estates, but provincial towns are referred to as "N", "S", "X", or ** — another arch but conventional method of suggesting that real towns are referred to, but the author deems it proper to preserve their anonymity.

In this way an all-purpose formula was created by Turgenev, which he re-used in all his novels and in many of the tales. An aura of apparent actuality is created by scrupulous observation of the rules of the game. 'On such and such a day', the formula goes, 'in a place we had better not name, though you know it well, such and such a person met so-and-so...'. And then, before things become too hectic, or indeed at all active, we are supplied with the background material needed for a rounded under-standing of both such and such a person and so-and-so. When the whole story is over the narrator is in no hurry to take his leave. He will not do so without satisfying the last demands of the reader's curiosity concerning the future lives of the characters he has come to know so well. At every stage in every novel Turgenev obeys these rules. They are self-imposed limitations which now look old-fashioned and unsophisticated but they serve Turgenev well, binding his novels into unified creations and setting them up persuasively as apparent pieces of reality by suggesting a broad and deep perspective of time and a rich sequence of events stretching well beyond the confines of the novels.

Turgenev's thoroughness in the application of this formula can scarcely be exaggerated. Nor can his predominating interesting in characters, rather than action or plot. The story-line always gave Turgenev trouble. Having conceived a series of authentic characters, he had to work hard to invent interesting activities to occupy them. He regarded as forbidden territory the extremes of abnormality and monomania, the murder and violence and the profound philosophical speculation used by other novelists to captivate their audience. Instead he directed his protagonists into unhappy affairs of the heart. All six novels describe an unsuccessful love-match, except *Smoke* which reunites the lovers, late in the day, in a virtual epilogue. Usually there is some kind of socio-political interest which adds both to the action and the significance of the novel. *Fathers and Sons* outranks the other five novels in a number of ways, but an increase in sheer activity is not one of them. There are some lively clashes of personality, temperament, and attitude, one or two love stories, even a rather forced and ineffectual duel and a death scene. This is, perhaps, a greater sum of activity than in, say, *Rudin*, but hardly more than in *A Nest*

of Gentlefolk which contains the sensational return from the dead of
Varvara Pavlovna, or in *Virgin Soil*, which has more bustle and a greater
tension and which culminates in a death scene of stronger dramatic impact
than that of Bazarov. All Turgenev's novels put the portrayal of character,
the evocation of atmosphere and the consideration of moral situations well
ahead of action, and *Fathers and Sons* is not distinctive in this respect.

On the other hand, this novel clearly deals with relationships of far
greater complexity than before or after, and there appears to be a greater
number of such relationships. To begin with, the love situations are
multiplied. At least three love-matches, all very different, occupy our
attention in the foreground, and this is to say nothing of the past
love-affairs of the two Kirsanov brothers, with Masha and Princess R.
Nikolai entertains a deep affection for Fenichka, part paternal, part
sexual, in no sense a threat to the hallowed memory of his first wife,
Masha. Arkadii begins and develops, despite himself and somewhat to his
own confusion, a perfectly orthodox romance with Katya. Of overriding
interest is the destruction of Bazarov by the force of love which he had
repudiated as merely a question of biological sexuality in Chapter VII but
which overwhelms him by Chapter XVIII and makes him exclaim to
Odintsova: 'There you are, then. I love, you, stupidly, madly. You see
what you've managed to do?'[5]

This is one of the strangest and most complex of Turgenev's love
relationships, involving a *volte-face* on the part of both protagonists.
Forced by circumstances to be clever, sensible, inscrutable, even
hard-hearted, Odintsova had never known happy relations with a man,
despite her acknowledged beauty and charm. She had sufficient youth left
in her to make falling in love still a real possibility; indeed she appeared
ripe for that very eventuality. Without a doubt she encouraged Bazarov
and brought him to the point of his declaration before retreating into
frigidity. While the circumstances seemed propitious, Odintsova's
temperament prevented her from falling in love. With Bazarov, it is quite
the reverse. Temperamentally he was opposed to the very idea of falling in
love. He did not acknowledge love's existence. He was a self-confessed,
unrepentant, inveterate egoist, independent, embarrassed by human
attachments, a lonely person, not merely enjoying solitude but dedicated
to it. Yet sheer circumstances made him fall in love. The strange interplay
of temperament and circumstance, and the rapid development of the
love-relationships in three successive chapters (XV, XVI, XVII) make
this section the climax of the novel and invest it with an element of
mystery and surprise which, for Turgenev, must count as an unusual
achievement. There is a real sense of these characters playing with forces
which they do not understand and cannot control. The hasty, uncertain,
unwanted and inevitably unhappy love-relationship between Bazarov and
Odintsova is thrown into relief by the banality of the one between two

much more ordinary and younger people, Arkadii and Katya, whom temperament and circumstance will bring together in a conventional union.

Although the love-stories of *Fathers and Sons* are more varied and complicated than is usual for Turgenev and therefore possess greater interest and meaning, they do not take over the whole novel. Far from it: Bazarov meets Odintsova, and Arkadii Katya, in Chapter XV, the first chapter of the second half of the novel. Before that we have had to content ourselves, for love-interest, with the understated, mild complexities of the Nikolai-Fenichka affair. Then, after Chapter XVIII, when Bazarov leaves Nikolskoe, Odintsova departs from the novel, to reappear only in the last three chapters (excluding Chapter XXVIII which is an untitled epilogue). Thus, the main female protagonist appears in only half-a-dozen chapters out of twenty-seven. It is clear that the love-interest occupies only a relatively small part of *Fathers and Sons*, and that there must be something greater than this filling the other twenty-two chapters. This greater ingredient is, of course, Bazarov himself, for whom a defeat on the field of love is no more than one important contest in a whole series of confrontations, from almost all of which he emerges as the loser, and which together add up to his total stature and condition — those of a tragic hero, no less.

It is important to view Bazarov in this light. This is how Turgenev saw him — not merely as an odd character unable to adjust to his society and surroundings, not merely as an originative, if sadly unsuccessful theoriser struggling to make himself heard, but as a tragic hero. In a letter to Sluchevsky of April 1862 Turgenev stated firmly: 'The qualities given to Bazarov are not accidental. I wanted to make a tragic figure out of him. There was no place for tenderness here.'[6] By general acknowledgement he succeeded, which is why Bazarov dwarfs everyone else, both in *Fathers and Sons* and in all of Turgenev's other novels and stories. The quality of *Fathers and Sons* rests upon this fact. How and why did Turgenev achieve success?

The two general qualities which a tragic hero must possess by definition are the ability to attract sympathy and the inability to avoid extreme suffering. Neither of these demanding capacities is beyond Bazarov. Turgenev must have sensed this in the prototype doctor whom he claimed to have met by chance on a rail journey (though the germ of the novel actually entered his mind while he was sea-bathing at Ventnor on the Isle of Wight). Turgenev was to remain commendably loyal to his original conception of Bazarov. He would resolutely refuse to alter his outlines when asked to do so before publication and with equal determination he was to reject most of the generally absurd *post factum* assessments of the elusive protagonist of his major novel. Such a wide range of assessments, both of the novel as a whole and specifically of Bazarov, constitutes a tribute to the work through an indication of its open-endedness.

Bazarov was evidently invested with ambiguity from the outset. This was deliberate and even unavoidable. He was such a huge figure, and so original, that even the author looked upon him as an enigma, finding it difficult to determine which were his good qualities, which were his bad ones and how they balanced out. To the poet Fet he wrote: 'Did I want to abuse Bazarov or extol him? I *do not know that myself*, since I don't know whether I love or hate him.'[7] So Bazarov is neither a villain nor a hero, but simply a new force, little understood at that time, but fascinating to observe in its early stages. If Bazarov is so ambiguous, how is it possible to say that he is sympathetic?

Certainly Bazarov has the ability to infuriate. He is rude to many people, asking bluntly for food when he has only just arrived, lounging about, yawning in mid-conversation, ignoring most of the social decencies, arguing and insulting without restraint. This is all on the surface, though it means that Bazarov makes a disconcerting impression on those who meet him. At a more profound level he may be seen as an uncompromising theorist who will not bend his ideas to fit in with anyone else's, perhaps a negativist who does not want to see the inherent dangers in his philosophy (which would lead one day to the violence of the latter-day nihilists, as Pavel Petrovich predicted). On the one hand, then, Bazarov appears rude, wrong-headed, foolish and potentially dangerous.

There is, however, much more to be said on the other side. Consider his rudeness. He is rude only to those people whom he sees as the enemies of his philosophy, the useless or pernicious parts of society and the empty-headed hangers-on in his own movement. He is not rude to Fenichka, nor to the peasant boys who catch frogs for him, and he is not condescending to carriage-drivers. With all of these he jokes and immediately sets up a pleasant rapport. As far as he is able he suppresses his impatience with his own doting parents. His rudeness is no mere eye-catching affectation but a consciously employed weapon in his single-handed battle for the restoration of true human values in society.

Bazarov's theories, however negative, have something to commend them. They are original, not the diluted philosophy of other men's minds. They are consistently adhered to in so far as it is humanly possible. They are well-intended. Bazarov wants little or nothing for himself; he seeks a totally new form of society that will be fair for everyone. He is open and honest. He is impatient with the ineffectiveness of earlier socio-political theories, which he sees as woolly-minded liberal idealism.

As a person Bazarov has an unusually compelling presence. No one can ignore him. He forces a reaction from everyone he meets, and people are changed by having met him. They become fawning disciples, fascinated onlookers or implacable enemies, but they are invariably stirred to thought and action. After one long argument (in Chapter XI) Nikolai Kirsanov is forced to reappraise his whole way of life. Bazarov is the enemy of complacency and represents an indispensable force which is needed to prompt consciences and insist on new thinking to improve the human condition. Despite his love of theory he is a pragmatist in everyday life, liking his food and a good cigar, enjoying his work, and possessing a natural common touch which immediately impresses ordinary people. On the credit side, then, he is original, compelling, consistent, well-meaning and honest.

The attitude adopted towards Bazarov by Turgenev (and probably by the reader) vacillates between attraction and repulsion. How much more worth-while and fascinating he is than the lumbering, single-minded Insarov, the hero of *On the Eve*, who preceded him by a few months. Only very gradually (if at all) are we won over to Bazarov by repeated subtle assertions of his altruism, sincerity and popularity with those (like children and peasants) who would immediately detect a single note of humbug or condescension. We cannot fail to admire the way in which he remains true to himself despite several defeats as the picture of his tragic situation emerges.

His tragedy is many-sided. First of all, Bazarov is out of place and ahead of his time. His whole training and natural outlook were unsuited to his age. He belongs more properly to a classless, technological society nearer to which the twentieth century has moved. More than that, he devoted his life to, and constructed his personality upon theories which were, one by one, disproved before his very eyes and the destruction of which totally undermined his existence. He is a sad reminder of the truth so often expounded in Russian literature that happiness comes from living rather than theorising about existence. Theory is a deadening influence. The failure of Bazarov is complete and it is painful to watch. He sets himself up as the champion of reason and loses every battle fought in the name of that faculty. He wins no converts to his cause who are worth converting. He repudiates old-fashioned concepts such as chivalry, yet allows himself to be drawn into fighting a duel. He scorns human affection, but has to fight hard to suppress his friendly love for Arkadii and his filial love for his excellent parents. He rejects love between men and women, but finds himself in love with Odintsova. He naturally rejects religion and yet consents to receive the last rites of the Church.

His death is the final irony. A trained physician, whose job it is to control nature by curing illness and who is theoretically impervious to simple disease, he is nevertheless struck down in his physical prime by a practical failure, the omission of an ordinary precautionary measure, the cauterisation of a wound when carrying out a *post mortem* examination on a man who had died from typhus. The death of Bazarov has been considered an arbitrary ending. Mirsky says that Turgenev 'lets him die, not from any natural development in the nature of the subject, but by the blind decree of fate'.[8] That is much truer of Insarov than of Bazarov. Bazarov's career is a whole series of ironic confrontations between theory and practice; each time practice comes out on top and his death (without our even considering the Freudian possibilities of a death-wish expressing itself in Bazarov's rather improbable negligence) may be seen as a most suitable culmination to these increasing ironies. It is artistically inevitable (in order to martyrise Bazarov into a tragic hero) and carried through with appropriate determination by Turgenev.

Bazarov is the one great force that lifts *Fathers and Sons* high above Turgenev's other novels. He is a gigantic literary creation, pressing into the forefront of the reader's consciousness from his first introduction by a rather awe-struck Arkadii, a dominating presence in almost every chapter from then on, and a haunting, disturbing reality even when he disappears for solitary walks or sits back to listen to a long account by Arkadii. If we knew exactly what he was, or how to appraise what he stood for, if the author gave us more clues towards determining an attitude to Bazarov, then he would begin to stiffen into the stolid simplicity of Insarov. But he is ambiguous, open-ended, invested with mystery and irony. Significantly, there is no detailed biography of Bazarov. Turgenev achieves objectivity, towards which he had to strive because of his own uncertainty, by defining Bazarov not through the easily assimilated method of digressive flash-back, but through hints and allusions and a gradual revelation of character in a series of fleeting confrontations, with Nikolai, with coachmen, with Pavel, with peasant lads and with Fenichka. There is no risk of over-exposure. A swift exchange of words, a few seconds for his interlocutor to assimilate a first impression of Bazarov and the hero is whisked away into a new situation. The veil is drawn back across him and someone else is described until another corner comes to be lifted. His first clash is delayed until Chapter VI, when he returns from frog-catching and is taunted into a response by Pavel Petrovich. The confrontation is allowed to last for some three pages only, and it is followed by a long, detailed biographical flashback, not of Bazarov, but of Pavel Petrovich (Chapter VIII). Turgenev gives Bazarov full rein for the first and only time in Chapter X, a third of the way through and the early climax to the novel, after which he closes the first act, relaxes the tensed spring and moves the action elsewhere.

There is, in short, a control and restraint in the presentation of Bazarov which add to his air of mystery and his fascination.

From the character of Bazarov many of the other merits of *Fathers and Sons* may be seen to flow. The question of the structure of the novel, which has worried a number of critics, is scarcely open to greater doubt than the also questioned appropriateness of Bazarov's death. *Fathers and Sons* contains a complex series of antitheses which Turgenev keeps in balance by his lack of commitment — or, to state it more affirmatively, his objectivity — and also by his judicious placing of characters within the general framework. The main antithesis, as reflected in the title, is between the generations, that is between the old and the young, between idealist and materialist philosophies, not between reaction and radicalism, but between old-fashioned and new-fashioned liberalism. Yet there are fascinating contrasts, both between Nikolai Petrovich and Pavel Petrovich and between Bazarov and Arkadii, who are supposed to belong to the same sides. All through the novel the characters pair off, contrast with each other and yet combine to present a different, shared face which will be contrasted against another dual grouping: Nikolai and Pavel, Bazarov and Arkadii, Odintsova and Katya, Sitnikov and Kukshina, Bazarov's two parents, the two lovers of Nikolai, the dead Masha and the living Fenichka, even down to the two different servants at Marino, Pyotr and Prokofich. It is like a complicated mobile. One pair of opposite polarities, themselves a fascinating comparison, acts as a counterpoise to another, and all the time the groups swing round, changing position and altering relationships, without ever throwing the whole scheme out of balance. This system of counterpoised dualities runs right through *Fathers and Sons*; it is held in equilibrium by the determined objectivity of Turgenev and it explains the harmony of the work, a harmony achieved nowhere else in his series of novels.

Such is the structure of *Fathers and Sons* with regard to the *dramatis personae*. As far as the events are concerned, *Fathers and Sons* is a peripatetic work; it moves backwards and forwards between the three homes of the Kirsanovs, Odintsova and Bazarov's parents. But this is no disadvantage. To begin with, the unity of the novel is never in question because of the constant presence and centripetal force of Bazarov himself (just as the rambling adventures of picaresque heroes like Lazarillo de Tormes, Gil Blas and Don Quixote are bound tightly together by the ever-present, ever-fascinating central hero). Secondly, the movement is turned to advantage. On the one hand a change of atmosphere means a reduction in tension (and this is an important part of the astute sense of timing displayed by Turgenev) and on at least one occasion it has symbolic value, when in Chapter XXII Arkadii goes back to Nikolskoe alone, leaving Bazarov behind and emphasising the real rift that has been opening between them and which becomes obvious in their argument in Chapter XXI. On the other hand the movement into new situations is necessary in order to expose the nihilists and their beliefs to new people and new events. In this way we not only extend and round off our knowledge of Bazarov and Arkadii, but we also watch their principles take the strain, bend and crack, as both of them see their theories mercilessly disproved.

These theories are of vital importance. They form the socio-political content of the novel. That there is such a content, and that it is a strong element, is undeniable, as is witnessed by the violent contemporary reaction and the pleasure *Fathers and Sons* afforded even such demanding critics as Dobrolyubov and Pisarev. Turgenev's novel became immediately celebrated, not for its literary qualities, but for its accuracy, or otherwise, in depicting new movements on the social scene in repressed, mid-century Russia. His work has often been referred to by historians, politicians and sociologists with only a peripheral interest in literature. Their main concern has always been for the new ideas surfacing in Russian society in the reign of Alexander II, and specifically the theories of the so-called 'New Men' of the 1860s who subscribed to the view that an equitable form of society could not be worked out by any method short of rejecting the past in its entirety and beginning again with a *tabula rasa*. Everyone had his own idea about how this should be done, and about what should follow when the decks were completely cleared. Bazarov exemplifies the New Man in his earliest stages, even at the moment of birth, so it is not surprising that he has no coherent positive programme worked out.

In a later work, *What is to be done?* (1863) Chernyshevsky was to demonstrate how easy it is to descend into absurdity when writing a sociological treatise masquerading as a literary work. Turgenev, no doubt encouraged by the evidence of a sure touch in *Fathers and Sons*, would himself in *Virgin Soil* fail to reproduce a novel which could bear the weight of his own later political theorising. How did it come out right in *Fathers and Sons*? What does Mirsky mean when he says eloquently that '*Fathers and Sons* is Turgenev's only novel where the social problem is distilled without residue into art, and leaves no bits of undigested journalism sticking out?'[9]

The answer lies in proportion and manner of presentation. Although the love-interest is a major theme in *Fathers and Sons*, it occupies only a small part of the novel. On the other hand, nearly three quarters of the much longer work, *Virgin Soil*, is devoted predominantly to one theme, the theories and actions of the populists. The sociological theorising of *Fathers and Sons* is very different from that of *Virgin Soil* in that it stands with the love-interest as merely one of the compelling issues at stake in the novel. The depiction of nihilism and its adherents comes slowly, little by little. Nobody forces information or opinion on anyone, neither the characters on each other, nor the author on the reader. The unfolding is gradual, usually unobtrusive and allowed a rapid acceleration only once — in Chapter X. A sense of proportion, a sense of timing and a sense of restraint steer Turgenev between the Scylla of *What is to be done?* and the Charybdis of *Virgin Soil*.

Some of the novel's other merits deserve a brief mention. Turgenev's love of natural scenery is undiminished in *Fathers and Sons*; and indeed Arkadii's lack of true affinity for the nihilist cause is highlighted by his love for nature which is no less strong than his father's. Turgenev's minor characters are amongst the delights of the novel — Fenichka and her baby, Sitnikov and Kukshina, Bazarov's parents, Father Alexei, the servants, coachmen and serf-lads, all of them standing quietly in the background, enjoying that rounded conception, deep integration into the narrative and wealth of authenticity which show Turgenev at the peak of his powers. The author's sense of humour is also at a high point of development, ranging from the subtle, stinging ironies of Pavel Petrovich to the overt satire against Sitnikov and Kukshina and the down-to-earth amusement created by uncomprehending, uncouth peasant boys. Turgenev's restraint extends also to a tight rein upon sentimentality, which is relaxed only in the somewhat unfortunate last few paragraphs. Turgenev's dependence upon dialogue, his expert manipulation of conversation which stems from an undying love of the theatre and long experience in it, is yet another important feature of *Fathers and Sons*. These are some of the secondary properties of a most successful novel. They are all introduced and employed with assurance and tact, undoubtedly because they are no more than subsidiary parts of a happily conceived whole.

Fathers and Sons is, in summary, a remarkably harmonious novel. It succeeds in its complex task of uniting many antitheses in an intricate pattern, superimposing a grandiose literary creation — Bazarov — which provides a constant guarantee of unity, proceeding with restraint, maintaining objectivity, fascinating the reader with poignant ambiguities and, above all, rising above its time into universality. The reader is gently led to think in terms of reason versus instinct, Man versus Nature, calculation versus chance occurrence, and forced to consider the ultimate insignificance and impotence of even the strongest representatives of mankind.

NOTES

1. Ford Madox Ford, *The Critical Attitude*, Duckworth & Co., London, 1911, p.59.
2. A. Daudet, 'Tourguéneff' in *Thirty Years of Paris and of my Literary Life*, Routledge, London, 1893, p.338.
3. I. S. Turgenev, *Polnoe sobranie sochinenii i pisem v dvadtsati vos'mi tomakh*, Moscow-Leningrad, 1960-1968, VIII, p.221.
4. *P.S.S.*, VII, p.178.
5. *P.S.S*, VIII, p.299.
6. *P.S.S.*, IV (Pis'ma), p.379.
7. *P.S.S.*, IV (Pis'ma), p.371.
8. D.S. Mirsky, *A History of Russian Literature*, Routledge & Kegan Paul, London, 1960, p.194.
9. Mirsky, p.194.

54 *The Voice of a Giant*

FURTHER READING ON TURGENEV

Richard Freeborn, *Turgenev. The Novelist's Novelist*, Oxford University Press, Oxford, 1960.
Victor Ripp, *Turgenev's Russia. From Notes of a Hunter to Fathers & Sons*, Cornell University Press, Cornell, 1980.
Leonard Schapiro, *Turgenev. His Life and Times*, Oxford University Press, Oxford, 1978.

V

DOSTOEVSKY: NOTES FROM UNDERGROUND

Dostoevsky's *Notes from Underground*, published in 1864, is well-established among the classics of modern European literature. Nearly 100 years after its publication the American scholar Joseph Frank wrote:

> Few works in modern literature are more widely read or more often cited than Dostoevsky's *Notes from Underground*. The designation 'underground man' has entered into the vocabulary of the modern educated consciousness, and this character has now begun — like Hamlet, Don Quixote, Don Juan and Faust — to take on the symbolic stature of one of the great archetypal literary creations. No book or essay on the situation of modern culture would be complete without some allusion to Dostoevsky's figure. Every important cultural development of the last half-century — Nietzscheanism, Freudianism, Expressionism, Surrealism, Crisis Theology, Existentialism — has claimed the underground man as its own; and when he has not been adopted as a prophetic anticipation, he has been held up to exhibition as a luridly repulsive warning.[1]

Writing in 1961, Frank naturally did not include more recent intellectual developments such as Structuralism and Post-structuralism, but might well wish to add them in revising his text today. A Deconstructive analysis of *Notes from Underground* might prove the most fruitful of all, though the aim of this article is much more modest and is based upon common-sense notions of reading and writing.

However, if such diverse and widespread interest establishes *Notes from Underground*'s place in the modern European consciousness, it also illustrates how many ways there are of understanding and interpreting it. Many a reader senses intuitively that here is a statement of great importance for anyone who wants to come to terms with modern man's spiritual problems, but unless he is familiar with some or all of those movements mentioned by Frank, he may be at a loss to know exactly what to make of it. After all, in Part I of the work there is no story to fall back on. This first part strikes one rather as a sort of emotional and philosophical outpouring, the confession of a man who is sick in mind, unable to integrate with society, and obsessed with certain profound philosophical problems with which he cannot cope.

F.M. Dostoevsky 1821-81

The forty-year-old narrator is psychologically sick, and has been so since childhood. He is spiteful and petty, confused and self-contradictory. He has always felt an outsider (alienated from society as modern jargon has it); and because he has always found it so difficult to find his bearings in life, he has always been easy prey to fashionable intellectual attitudes. He cannot find a secure mooring in life on any level of his experience. He has no sense of the Holy (as Dostoevsky was to write some years later);[2] he is, as some critics have put it, a hollow man. Almost at the end of his notes, the Underground Man observes:

> We do not even know where living reality is now, what it is, or what it is called. Leave us alone without our wretched little books and we immediately grow confused and lose our way. We don't know what to adhere to, what to follow, what to love, what to hate, what to respect or what to despise. We even become weary of being human beings — human beings with their *own*, real flesh and blood...[3]

'Leave us alone without our books and we immediately grow confused and lose our way'. In Part II, where the narrator recalls his life at the age of twenty-four, it is Gogol, Nekrasov, Schiller, George Sand and composite fantasies from the Romantics, the Natural School and recent human history — particularly the age of Napoleon — that swarm in the Underground Man's mind. The motif of the wet snow is taken from the Natural School in whose works it often appeared; the epigraph is taken from Nekrasov; the ideal of *the sublime and the beautiful* is a late eighteenth-century concept to be found in the philosophy of Burke, of Kant, and most significant of all for Russia in the period of the 1840s, of the German poet, philosopher and dramatist, Schiller. The idea of the pure prostitute and the concept of acute sensibility as simultaneously a sign of superiority and a curse are both also well-known and widespread Romantic images.

Part I, when the narrator has reached the age of forty, is set in the 1860s, years marked first by the Great Reforms in Russia and then by the American Civil War and the Prussian seizure of Schleswig-Holstein, both of which leave a mark on the Underground Man's thought. Most important of all, however, a new set of ideas has taken possession of the Underground Man's mind. As one can see in retrospect, they have not altogether banished the old ideas, but it is these new ones, the creed of the progressives of the sixties, which have him in their thrall. The central figure in propagating this creed was Nikolai Chernyshevsky who at this time was incarcerated in the Peter and Paul fortress, but nonetheless had managed to publish an inflammatory novel, *What is to be done?* in 1863. Chernyshevsky was not merely a novelist; he was a philosopher and leader of progressive youth as well, and it is his ideas against which the Underground Man is rebelling even though he finds them irrefutable.

They are utilitarian, rationalist and determinist ideas, which, in the tradition of the Enlightenment, present man as an ultimately rational creature, who only has to be shown his true interests to act in accordance with them and who lives in a world, moreover, where rational laws prevail in the moral as well as the natural sphere, so that his individual freedom is severely restricted, if not altogether illusory. Among the complex of ideas which have taken the Underground Man's mind captive and which can be identified in the text are those of the French eighteenth-century philosopher Diderot, the French socialist Fourier, and more recently, those of Darwin, as published in his *On the Origin of Species* in 1859 and glossed by Huxley's *Man's Place in Nature* which had appeared in English in 1863 and in Russian translation in 1864. Similarly, there is a reference to the English writer H.T. Buckle, who for a time enjoyed a vogue among European intellectuals and the first volume of whose *History of Civilisation in England* was published in Russian translation in 1863.[4] In this work, Buckle had expressed the idea, from which the Underground Man dissents, that with the development of civilisation wars will cease.

Thus, the Man from Underground is up-to-date in his reading, but unfortunately he takes it all too personally. The first section of the narrator's notes probably does not strike the modern English reader as having very much to do with philosophy at all. Essentially it appears as the self-revelation of someone who is emotionally confused. But, in the second section, these introspective meanderings and complaints move in the direction of something recognisable as philosophy, with the narrator's ascription of his emotional problems to what he calls *the laws of consciousness*. He wants to understand and to explain why he feels pleasure in the knowledge that he is a scoundrel and in making other people uncomfortable; why he feels so many conflicting emotions doing battle within him; why he is spiteful and yet at the same time knows he is not really spiteful; why it is just at the moment when he is most sensitive to 'the sublime and the beautiful' that he does the most immoral things; why he feels such pleasure at his own degradation. The conclusion he comes to is that he is suffering from an excess of what he calls consciousness, of what we might perhaps call morbid, introspective reflection, and that this consciousness is subject to laws which deprive him of his free will. Whatever illusions he may have about acting in accordance with his ideal, or improving himself morally, these laws debar him from changing in any way. The man with an over-sensitive consciousness is tormented by ideals of goodness and beauty; yet he is lured into vice as well, and, finally, he knows that all this is completely beyond his control. Things will be as they will be. No-one is to blame for anything. None of this stops him from feeling his degradation, from smarting at insults or from dreaming of revenge; but he can never make up his mind to do anything because he knows that everything is subject to laws over which he has no control.

This, at least, is the explanation he offers. He feels impotent, and he suffers all the humiliation and rancour of impotence.

The Underground Man develops this theme in his third section of Part I: he describes how he sweats and stews and plots revenge, but in the end achieves nothing and has no alternative but to withdraw into his underground and seethe, until eventually he is forced to accept the inevitable. A stupid man, the man of action or the man of Nature as he has been called, understands none of this and so charges on regardless. If the man of action encounters an obstacle, a stone wall, he does not understand what stands in his way, but just steps aside, and consequently he is not subject to unhealthy brooding. He is representative of normality. But the man who reflects on the philosophical implications is rendered immobile. He knows he is impotent and he suffers from the feeling of impotence, and is resentful. Resentment is an important idea in the thought of some of the existentialists, notably Nietzsche.[5] Camus, for instance, quotes Scheler's definition that resentment is the evil secretion of prolonged impotence in a sealed vessel;[6] and this seems to be exactly what the Underground Man is talking about.

The only thing to do is to take it out on other people. In section IV, the narrator introduces his famous metaphor of the educated man with toothache, which expresses perfectly his situation. The educated man knows that he can do nothing about his toothache, that whether it goes or gets worse is subject to natural laws over which he has no control. In a sense he enjoys the consciousness that he is the plaything of such laws. But he makes other people suffer too by his groans and thereby obtains some relief from his suffering.

In the following sections of Part I the Underground Man takes some of these ideas further. He affirms that the result of excess consciousness is inertia and ennui. Stupid people jump easily to conclusions; intelligent people get lost in their own analyses and can never find a sufficient cause for any course of action. He has never been able to become anything positive.

It is clear that in his heart of hearts the Underground Man does not know whether he is a free agent or not. He cannot refute the modern deterministic concept of scientific law, but the fact that he is obsessed with his own freedom or lack of freedom indicates that many of his attitudes tacitly assume that what he is suffering from is not so much a law of nature as an emotionally based feeling of impotence and/or moral cowardice. This is his fundamental problem, around which the whole fiction is built.

Consequently he comes to question the validity of these so-called laws. He asks whether it is after all so obvious that if man were shown his own interests in accordance with some mathematical table, he would in fact act in accordance with them. Has man, he asks, in the whole of recorded history, ever behaved rationally, even when he understands the correct rational course? Man is irrational and perverse. At times it may even be of benefit to man to do something contrary to his interests as seen from the rational standpoint, and if this is true then it undermines all rational schemes for regulating man's activities.

The narrator runs through a series of well-known historical events; he glances at Buckle's questionable view of civilisation; he alludes to the martial activities of the two Napoleons; he mentions Schleswig-Holstein and the still-raging American Civil War, and finds little to support the view of man's rationality. Diderot may have believed that man is like an organ stop or a piano key, and science may teach that the laws of nature determine man's actions; logarithm tables may be worked out for every conceivable eventuality; the Crystal Palace may be built. But, if for no other reason than that he was bored, man would be certain to knock it down. The symbol of the Crystal Palace to represent an ideal, rationally ordered society derives in part from Dostoevsky's own visit in 1862 to the Crystal Palace at Sydenham, the centrepiece of Prince Albert's Great Exhibition, but even more from an episode in Chernyshevsky's novel *What is to be done?* where the image of the Crystal Palace represents the ideal of a technological utopia.[7]

No, the Underground Man concludes, the rationalists are wrong. Man is not ultimately rational. In all times and places men prefer to act as they choose rather than in accord with reason if the latter means sacrificing their individuality. Man prefers independent choice to a rational, comfortable existence.

But what if there is no such thing as independent choice? Here the Underground Man is brought back to the crux of his problem, and he replies that whereas reason may bring man to this conclusion, reason is only one of man's faculties. The faculty which represents the whole man is not reason, but will, and will says differently. This is the high point of his argument. The trouble is that he does not wholly believe this either, and he now resorts to arguments built not so much on confidence in his will or its freedom, as on a frenzied rebellion against the tyranny of reason. Man would rather do something perverse, or even go mad, than accept this tyranny. Man may be attracted by reason and creativity, but he is also attracted by chaos and destruction, perhaps because what he fears most of all is to bring his task to completion. Ants may behave in accordance with a mathematical model, but men are not ants. Twice-two-is-four may be very appealing to the reason, but twice-two-is-five has its fascination too. The Underground Man ultimately rejects the Crystal Palace, as he says memorably, because man cannot put out his tongue at it. But the narrator is exhausted by all this philosophising and the emotional toll which it takes, and sinks back into his Underground. Is this the best place after all, or is there something better for which he yearns?

The possibility that there might be something better than what the Underground Man calls the Underground relates to a passage which the censor refused to have in the text and which is now lost, but in which Dostoevsky intended to suggest the possibility of a Christian utopia, founded on love.

The Underground Man is certainly very unattractive, and no sane reader would choose the Underground as he does, but this is not really the point. Dostoevsky (as opposed to his narrator) is trying to convey something rather different. If it were true that man has no free will and this were to be appreciated by intelligent and sensitive beings, the kind of psychological predicament which would result would be the following: people with high ideals who were convinced that to realise such ideals was an impossibility and that they were the victims of inescapable laws would be reduced to an emotionally exhausting sense of impotence, against which they could protest only by caprice and perversity... In his foreword Dostoevsky even claimed that people like this already existed. The fundamental problem was by no means a new one, nor is it outdated, since it is easy to find parallels today. No solution is offered in *Notes from Underground*, but Dostoevsky was to try to formulate an answer in terms of Christianity in his later works.

Many commentators on Dostoevsky have argued that it is its ideological aspect which is the most important, but others have said that the Underground Man's philosophising seems to require some external explanation, since his own commentary is clearly unreliable. The most appropriate position to adopt, it has been argued, is the psychological one. 'Its every aspect,' one commentator has written of *Notes from Underground*, 'including the philosophical speculations of Part I and the way in which the material is ordered, is an expression of the Underground Man's psyche.'[8] This is undoubtedly true, though the two approaches to the work are far from incompatible. One of the central and most significant features of Dostoevsky's work is his intuitive understanding of the way that ideas and personalities interact.

It is therefore important to look more closely at the Underground Man's emotional problems and the way in which they dispose him to certain philosophical attitudes. His is, of course, a very complex personality. One can discern in him tendencies towards aggression and the assertion of intellectual and moral superiority. Yet there are also tendencies towards self-effacement, a sense of moral culpability and a conviction of his own inferiority. The Underground is above all a symbol of withdrawal. One notes a tendency in the hero to withdraw altogether from other people, from moral problems and from intellectual turmoil, opposed by a periodic desire to integrate himself with the common run of humanity and even to achieve a genuinely warm human relationship with another person.

This extremely complex emotional problem can be analysed in accordance with various psychological theories, but here only its main features can be indicated.[9]

The Underground Man's problems begin with an unloved childhood. Not only is he an orphan, but he arrives at school full of suspicion of everyone and is greeted by taunts and jibes because he is different from everyone else. His basic response is to withdraw into himself and to find some compensation for his failure to establish positive relationships with others in a consciousness of his own intellectual and aesthetic superiority. (Later, in his address to Liza, he comes to romanticise what he has missed).

Although he stands apart from his fellows, however, he still yearns for human fellowship; though he tries to ignore their taunts, they still wound him and make him yearn for revenge; though he scorns their vulgarity, he envies their social ease; though he wants to dominate others, he is discontented when he succeeds; though he cherishes high ideals, he senses their other-worldliness; though he scorns the values of the world, he is humiliated by his poverty and by the derision of others. He knows that social integration and acceptance is beyond him and at times he withdraws, in consciousness of the superiority of his own values. At other times he so desperately needs company that he is prepared to undergo humiliation, and even enjoys it up to a point. Or else, in an attempt to escape from inertia he takes refuge in a bout of debauchery.

The first few pages of Part II describe in some detail the young narrator's emotions and thoughts about his unhealthy withdrawal from others and about the extremes of self-deprecation and feelings of superiority which he experiences.

The first anecdote which he tells concerns the officer who brushes him aside like an insect as he leaves the billiard hall, and the torments which he undergoes as a consequence. His plans and fantasies reveal his many-sidedness to the full. He harbours a grudge for several years. Firstly, he writes a scurrilous tale which he intends to be published, then he composes a letter full of fine feelings but with the veiled threat of a duel in it. The article is not published, and the letter is not sent. Finally he wreaks his revenge after months and months of obsessive scheming by barging into the officer in the street in such a way that he is not even sure that the man has noticed. But what this episode shows most clearly of all is the state of mind suggested in Part I: the consequence of a feeling of impotence with regard to participation in the normal patterns of life. The whole affair is so completely out of proportion to its cause, so ludicrous in the hold it has taken on the narrator's imagination and the strain it imposes on his emotional resources, that it would be laughable if it were not so pathetic.

Then he tells of his withdrawal into Romantic dreams, and finally, he embarks on his recollections of the central episode in the second part, the story of Zverkov and Liza. This episode too displays all the Underground Man's problems: his desire to participate; his wish to impose himself as a superior spirit; his consciousness that he looks ridiculous; and his perverse pleasure in being humiliated. It displays too his delight in tormenting others, the basic hostility of his relationship with his so-called friends, his dreams of moral and aesthetic grandeur, and his readiness to take offence. We are taken through every detail of his confused and complex feelings, and of his interaction with Zverkov and his friends.

The Underground Man is just as repulsive and foolish at the meal to which he has invited himself as an unwelcome guest as he imagines he will be, and the result is predictable. He emerges in a state of turmoil, determined to restore his dignity in some fashion, and makes off for the brothel in pursuit of the rest of the party who have thankfully left him behind.

It is there that he meets Liza, and lectures her on the fate which awaits her if she pursues her profession much longer. All this he says as though reciting from a book, and this is more or less the truth, for he has indeed picked it up from books.

The psychological importance of his preaching is that, through it, he temporarily restores the sense of self-esteem which he had lost so disastrously at the dinner; and yet he is sowing the seeds of further disaster, for he does not really believe what he is saying. Although he draws on his own fantasy in what he says to Liza, he is on dangerous emotional ground, for he preaches love, a commodity which he cannot offer, but which he knows he desperately needs and lacks. This might, he senses, have been his salvation, but it is not, because when Liza later turns up at his house, catching him by surprise, he is humiliated by her finding him in his degraded and impoverished circumstances, and this brings out all his old impulses of vindictiveness and spite...He takes his revenge on her for momentarily reversing their positions, by making love to her and then offering her money as she leaves, as though that was what she had come for.

When she leaves and he cannot catch her he is filled with remorse and self-hatred, but there is nothing he can do. He is once again impotent, not only in regard to the world, but in his attempt to order his own personality. Nor is this feeling in any way alleviated in his relations with his surly and recalcitrant manservant, who, though limited in outlook, has learnt to tyrannise the Underground Man just as the latter tries to tyrannise others. The hero is aware of the nature of his problem, and he is aware that there is something much better which is inaccessible to him, but since it is inaccessible there is nothing but the Underground after all.

Once we have looked at the Underground Man as he remembers himself, certain aspects of his philosophy become clearer. It is obvious that he makes use of his reading of the Romantics in his fantasies and also in his sermon to Liza, which derives in part from such fantasy.

But it is no less clear that it is his sense of impotence, displayed most clearly in the adventure with the officer, which lays the emotional basis for his acceptance of 'scientific determinism' and the constraints which that places upon free will. Such a doctrine confirms his own intuition that nothing he does or resolves to do can alter his position of emotional confusion and alienation from society. That position seems to receive support from his own discovery that the more he ponders and reflects, the more complex life seems, the more his resolution is eroded, and the less capable he is of doing anything at all except nurse his bitterness and resentment.

Furthermore, if scientific determinism in this crude sense were true, it would remove from him all moral responsibility, for if free will is illusory, no-one can be blamed for his actions, and talk of good and evil becomes meaningless. Yet the idea of the sublime and the beautiful lingers on in his consciousness and he cannot remain completely satisfied with such a view of life.

If the Underground Man's proneness to accept 'scientific determinism' and all its implications can be understood in terms of emotional problems which already existed before he had read a word of Chernyshevsky, so too can his reaction in affirming his right to be perverse. This has, after all, always been his way of dealing with intractable problems. When in a tight corner, he has never managed to do what rationally might be in his best interests. The rational has never been completely dominant in his life. On the contrary, it would seem that his every waking moment (and perhaps his sleep too) has been filled with the irrational, or at least the non-rational: with dreams and fantasies, with plans of revenge, vindictiveness and spite, with sadistic and masochistic yearnings of one kind or another. When he is already making himself ridiculous with Zverkov, he persists in plunging ever deeper into an inextricable morass of embarrassment and unnecessary discomfort. When he has an opportunity to establish a rapport with someone who understands and pities him, he reacts by destroying the burgeoning relationship. There is little that can be called rational here.

So the Underground Man's philosophical attitudes are rooted not only in contemporary cultural and philosophical views, but also in his own personality disorder. In trying to resolve the philosophical question he is also trying to resolve his spiritual problems, and in both he fails.

Of course, this identity of personal and philosophical is characteristic of much modern existentialist thought. For the existentialists, the primary problems are the problems of the individual brought face to face with the reality of living, that is of acting rather than observing. The existentialist philosopher is not one to stand on the touchline and assume a position of objectivity and impassivity. He is involved, or *engagé* as Sartre has it. Walter Kaufmann is surely right when he says that although there is no reason for calling Dostoevsky an existentialist, Part I of *Notes from Underground* is the best overture for existentialism ever written.[10]

NOTES

1. Joseph Frank. 'Nihilism and *Notes from Underground*', *Sewanee Review*, LXIX, 1961, p.1.
2. F.M. Dostoevskii, *Polnoe sobranie sochinenii v tridtsati tomakh*, Leningrad, 1972- , XVI, p.330.
3. *P.S.S.*, V, pp.178-179.
4. For further details see, *inter alia*, Joseph Frank.
5. Friedrich Nietzsche, *The Genealogy of Morals*.
6. Albert Camus, *The Rebel*, Penguin, Hardmondsworth, 1975, p.23.
7. N.G. Chernyshevskii, *Polnoe sobranie sochinenii v pyatnadtsati tomakh*, Moscow, 1939-1950, XI, p.277.
8. Bernard J. Paris, 'Notes from Underground; a Horneyan Analysis', PMLA, LXXXVIII, 1973, p.511.
9. For example, Bernard J. Paris.
10. Walter Kaufmann, *Existentialism from Dostoevsky to Sartre*, Meridian Books, Cleveland, 1956, p.14.

FURTHER READING ON DOSTOEVSKY

Malcolm V. Jones, *Dostoyevsky. The Novel of Discord*, Paul Elek, London, 1976.
William J. Leatherbarrow, *Fedor Dostoevsky*, Twayne Publishers, NY, 1981.
Richard Peace, *Dostoyevsky: an Examination of the Major Novels*, Cambridge University Press, Cambridge, 1971.

L.N. Tolstoy 1828-1910

VI

TOLSTOY: WAR AND PEACE

The first and most obvious characteristic of *War and Peace* is its size. Well over one thousand pages long, with an astonishing range of theme, character and situation, it occupies a very special place in modern Western literature. When it first appeared in full in 1869, contemporary reviews were by no means all favourable. The standard opinion seemed to be that, although there was much in the work that revealed the hand of a genius, it suffered, taken as a whole, from the defects of its size: part-novel and part-treatise, it lacked organic wholeness, aesthetic shape or a central unifying idea. This line of criticism is best summed up in Henry James's famous characterisation of *War and Peace* as a 'loose, baggy monster'.[1] In another context he referred to Tolstoy, together with Dostoevsky, as 'fluid pudding',[2] implying a somewhat incongruous mixture of looseness and indigestibility.

For even the most fervent admirer of Tolstoy it would be difficult not to find at least some truth in these accusations. *War and Peace* clearly has not the aesthetic balance or shape of the more conventional nineteenth-century novel; neither the opening nor the conclusion seem to be planned in any way, and the narrative flow of the text is interrupted by the author's prolix, dogmatic and often tedious philosophising.

The inference, however, that Tolstoy spent little care or preparation over the composition of his novel and wrote without paying much attention to its form and architecture is unjustified. It took in fact seven years to write — between 1863 and 1869 — and underwent numerous drafts and revisions. The opening scene alone — at Madame Scherer's salon — passed through fifteen draft versions before Tolstoy approved of it sufficiently for publication.

Two points in particular should be remembered in connection with the genesis of *War and Peace*: firstly, Tolstoy, when he started work on the novel, had very little idea of what he wanted to say. Like Dostoevsky's novels, *War and Peace* emerged as it was written, a slow and sometimes painful process of birth. And, as with Dostoevsky, the finished product bore only a faint resemblance to the original sketches. Starting off with vague ideas of a novel about the Decembrists, Tolstoy's attention became more and more focussed on the time when the generation of the Decembrists was being formed, and particularly on that crucial, traumatic year of 1812, the year of Napoleon's invasion of Russia. This led him in

turn to look further back in Russian history to the years when Russia
suffered defeat and shame at the hands of Napoleon, thus putting the
victory of 1812 into sharper perspective. The title of the novel changed
with its development, passing from *The Decembrists*, to *1805*, to the insipid
All's Well That Ends Well and finally, at a relatively late stage, to the
all-embracing arrogance of *War and Peace*.

Secondly, *War and Peace* was Tolstoy's first major work. With
hindsight it can be seen that all the themes and ideas in his earlier works
such as *Childhood* (1852), with its freshness and immediacy of
characterisation, sensuous description and psychological insight, his
Sevastopol Sketches (1855–56) which revealed his abomination of war and
contempt for government, *Family Happiness* (1859) with its somewhat
crude didacticism and analysis of family life, *The Cossacks* (1863) with its
Rousseauesque faith in nature and natural man, uncorrupted by
civilisation, were to flow into the material for *War and Peace*. But in the
latter they are combined and integrated to form an artistic whole.

Indeed the argument of this essay is precisely that *War and Peace*,
despite the strictures and reservations, does constitute an artistic whole.
The novel coheres in a very special way, and we can begin to understand
why this should be by examining something Tolstoy himself wrote à
propos of *Anna Karenina*, but which could refer equally well to *War and
Peace*:

> If I wanted to express in words everything that I had in mind to
> express in the novel I should have to write the very novel that I have
> written all over again...In everything, in almost everything I wrote I
> was guided by the need to collect ideas, linked together, for
> expressing myself, but each idea, expressed in words on its own, loses
> its meaning and is terribly reduced when it is taken on its own out of
> the linking where it is found. This linking is formed not I think by
> ideas but by something else, and to express the basis of this linking
> directly in words is impossible; it can only be done indirectly, by
> words describing images, actions and situations.[3]

Tolstoy achieves this internal linking primarily by the use of two devices
— repetition and contrast, and these in turn are achieved by very strict
control of his material. It is one of the paradoxes of Tolstoy's art that, for
the most part, he is able to convey the illusion of naturalness and freedom,
while at the same time retaining absolute control. To few other writers
does the principle of 'the art that conceals art' apply so precisely.

The most basic contrast in the novel is implicit in the title itself, *War
and Peace*. Put at its simplest, Tolstoy is concerned with the conflict and
contrast between, on the one hand, those forces which have their impulse
towards destruction and death — death, in the widest sense, including
death of the spirit — and, on the other, those forces which have their

impulse towards life. Indeed, it could be argued that all the various forms of contrast which Tolstoy adopts in *War and Peace* are, directly or indirectly, expressions of this basic contrast which forms the most important, if hidden, span of the novel's construction.

If war entails not only death and destruction but also an irruption into the private lives of countless thousands of ordinary individuals, peace above all means continuity, the continuity of life. Tolstoy goes to great lengths to stress this point: that despite the manipulation of governments, dictators, generals, ministers and emperors, the flow of life continues unchecked. Notice, for example, Tolstoy's description of life in Voronezh at the very height of the war with the French:

> At a time when Russia was half overrun by invaders and the inhabitants of Moscow were escaping to the provinces and group after group of volunteers were rising to defend their homeland, it is natural for those of us who were not living then to imagine that every Russian, great or small, was engaged solely in sacrificing himself, saving his fatherland, or weeping over its downfall. The tales and descriptions of that time speak only of self-sacrifice, love for the fatherland, despair, grief and Russian heroism. In reality this was not so. We imagine it to be so only because we see the general historic interest of that time and fail to see all the private, personal interests of individual people. Yet in reality those personal interests so transcend the general interest that they always prevent the public interest from being felt or even noticed. The majority of people at that time paid no attention at all to the general progress of events but were guided simply by their private interests, and they were the very people whose activities were the most useful.[4] (IV.I.4)*

This last point is made many times in the course of the novel and forms one of the links between the 'war' episodes and the 'peace' episodes; we are confronted by a typically Tolstoyan paradox that the less conscious a person is of the course of events, the more useful his actions are.

The tension between change and continuity is applied by Tolstoy not just to life in general but also to individual lives. If we follow the lives of the heroes, Pierre, Prince Andrew, Princess Mary, Nikolai and Natasha Rostov, we see that although each of them changes in important respects, they nevertheless stay recognisably the same. This remains true even if we include the first *Epilogue*, set in 1820 when fifteen years have elapsed since the novel's opening scene. Natasha has changed the most: with her, in the *Epilogue*, Tolstoy applies his technique, in an almost perverse manner, of 'making it strange' — that is, stripping an object of its familiar associations

---

* The three figures in brackets refer to the volume (book), part and chapter of *War and Peace* in which the quotation can be found. Most standard editions of the novel, in both Russian and English, are now divided in this way.

and presenting it directly, in almost crude terms. If the Natasha of the *Epilogue* does come as a shock the other characters all retain, to a greater or lesser extent, their essential selves from the main body of the novel. The *Epilogue* forms not just an appendix but the final strand in an intricately woven web, an intermeshing of time, space and human consciousness. It is not by chance that Tolstoy puts the final thoughts in Part I of the *Epilogue* into the head of the young Nicholas Bolkonsky, the very same child with whom Princess Lise was pregnant in the opening scene of the novel.

Of all the major fictional characters, if we exclude Platon Karataev, only one, Prince Andrew Bolkonsky, the father of young Nicholas, does not live to see the *Epilogue*. It is Prince Andrew who above all embodies the novel's fundamental contrasting 'dualism': the oscillation between life and death. As we trace his progress through the course of the novel he seems to swing like a pendulum between the extremes of hope and hopelessness, between a joyous realisation that life is meaningful and a resigned sense that all is vanity and meaninglessness. Each of the climactic moments in his life — Austerlitz, the death of his wife, the meeting with Pierre at Bogucharovo, his relationship with Natasha, Borodino — serves to push him in one direction or the other. At no stage does Andrew, unlike Pierre who undergoes similar crucial and formative experiences, seek consciously for the meaning of life; his fundamental impulse, on the contrary, is towards the lodestar of death. Certainly the awareness of death as an almost physical presence, even when he is apparently most oriented towards life, is never far away from his thoughts; and it is death which emerges as the final victor. Lying wounded after Borodino, he dreams of his own death:

> But at the very moment he died Prince Andrew remembered that he was asleep and that very same moment, making an effort, he woke up.
> 'Yes, that was death. I died – I awoke. Yes, death is an awakening'. His whole being became suffused with an inner radiance and the veil concealing the unknown was lifted from his spiritual vision. [5] (IV.I.16)

For Prince Andrew then, death becomes an awakening from life and from love. From a different perspective, however, Prince Andrew's death is not an awakening but a renunciation. The ambivalent tone of this passage is a reflection of Tolstoy's difficulties with the characterisation of his hero; it shows also that, at the time of writing *War and Peace*, he was too full of a sense of life and its creative powers to allow the concept of renunciation to become dominant.

For Andrew it is Natasha Rostova who is the focal point and embodiment of such positive forces. If it is love for her which renews and invigorates his spirit after the shattering experiences of Austerlitz and the death of his wife, then it is her betrayal of him which forces the return to cynicism, world-weariness, and preoccupation with death. It is Natasha Rostova, too, who shines like a star in Pierre's consciousness and whom he eventually marries.

In this way it is possible to place Natasha, as the embodiment of the life-giving force, at the very centre of the novel. But Natasha of course does not exist in isolation: she exists as part of a family. It is through the Rostovs above all that Tolstoy makes us aware of the importance of the family as a life-enhancing force. It is for them that Tolstoy reserves his most magical and poetical moments and episodes: Natasha's nameday party, the family joy and celebration as Nikolai returns home on leave, the hunt, the evening at Uncle's, the mummers and the troika ride. It is a family characterised by sensitivity, love, and close and immediate understanding of each other. Those members who share these feelings form a privileged group of people who are fundamentally contrasted with others, outsiders, who are unable to participate. Sonya, who is both part of the family and yet outside it, can live only a kind of surrogate existence:

> Sonya, as always, refrained from joining in although they all shared the same memories. Sonya did not remember much of what they remembered; but even what she *did* remember did not inspire in her the same poetic feeling which *they* experienced. She merely took pleasure in their joy, trying to imitate it.[6] (III, IV, 10)

Throughout the work there is a clear dividing-line drawn between those who, like the Rostov family, lead lives which are spontaneously natural and unforced and those who lead lives which are counterfeit or made false, either through lack of personal qualities or by a deliberate renunciation of their true selves for purposes of self-advancement. An example of the latter is Boris Drubetskoy, the boyhood friend of Nikolai Rostov, with whom he is throughout contrasted. But Tolstoy reserves his most devasting attitude for the Bergs, concerned more with their place in society than with having children. The Bergs' crime, in Tolstoy's eyes, is not their self-centredness — the Rostovs, after all, are equally self-centred; they are condemned for their artificiality and lack of spontaneity. In just the same way Natasha's qualities are brought into greatest relief when measured against those of her elder sister Vera:

> But Vera's face did not become any prettier when she smiled; on the contrary, her face took on an unnatural and therefore unpleasant expression. The elder girl, Vera, was a pretty, clever girl, a diligent well-brought-up person with a pleasant voice, everything she said was balanced and to the point; but, strange to say, everyone present looked round at her as if astonished at what she had just said and felt ill at ease.[7] (I.I.12)

The central turning-point of *War and Peace* — the episode of Natasha's abortive affair with Anatole Kuragin — comes almost exactly half-way through the novel, at the end of Volume II. It is an episode which affects the characters' lives radically. After the failure of the attempted elopement Anatole is forced to leave Moscow: ahead of him lie service in the army, Borodino, the horrible pain of amputation and death. Natasha herself is emotionally broken and does not recover for several months, but in those few months she turns from a girl into a young woman. (We should notice, incidentally, the characteristically Tolstoyan irony that the signal for her complete recommitment to life is the news of the death of her younger brother, Petya.)

The affair is of decisive importance in Natasha's relationship with both Prince Andrew and Pierre. On the one hand, it casts Prince Andrew back to the edge of the abyss; on the other, it makes Pierre fully aware for the first time of his feelings for Natasha. In a moving moment at the very end of Volume II, distraught almost to the point of suicide, she tells Pierre that all is lost:

> 'Everything lost?' Pierre repeated. 'If I were not the person I am but the handsomest, cleverest and finest person in the world and were free to do so, I would go down on my knees this instant and ask you for your hand and your love'.[8] (II.V.22)

But when we explore the reasons for Natasha's behaviour during this episode we see that here too Tolstoy is concerned to emphasise the importance of family life and family ties. We should not forget the effect of the forced separation from Prince Andrew on Natasha, nor the impact which the handsome and self-assured Anatole, together with his beautiful but empty sister Hélène, makes on her. Then there is the opera, whose powerful but corrupt and artificial influence acts like a drug on her mind. Tolstoy uses all these factors to prepare the ground carefully for Natasha's impetuous involvement with Anatole. But there is one more reason, the decisive one; just at the time the affair is coming to a climax the Rostovs are not together as a family, Nicholas has rejoined his regiment, and old Count Rostov has had to leave Moscow for two crucial days. Most importantly of all, Natasha's mother has had to stay behind in the country as she is unwell. Tolstoy takes great pains throughout the book to stress the close relationship between mother and daughter, and now, when Natasha needs help and advice most of all, there is nobody for her to turn to. There is only Sonya, but she, as we have already seen, is an outsider. The point is clear: Tolstoy saw family life as the source from which all truly moral behaviour flows; separation from such family life leads to falsehood, deception and betrayal. On a larger scale, the end of family life can signify the destruction of a nation.

The Rostov family then stands at the very centre of *War and Peace* in that its members, both individually and as a group, embody those spiritual and emotional qualities which Tolstoy most wished to convey. Its significance becomes clear if we translate the terms of the novel's title — war and peace — into death and life, for each of the Rostovs, with the exception of Vera, possesses those life-enhancing attributes which form the central pillar of Tolstoy's philosophy: simplicity, naturalness and spontaneity. The Rostovs represent a moral criterion by which all the other characters in the novel stand or fall. It is in them that the crucial importance of private life, as opposed to the public life (and spiritual death) of the Court, society and the St Petersburg salon world, is most fully revealed. Taken as a whole, *War and Peace* can be seen as a reflection of the dualism inherent in its author; it reveals, on the one hand, Tolstoy's need for a rational system of explanation; and, on the other hand, his instinctive recognition that life transcends, spills over the boundaries of reason. It is through the Rostovs above all that he is able to reaffirm his belief in the constant regeneration of life, in the links between the temporal and the eternal and therefore his faith in mankind's ultimate redemption. Beside this declaration of faith, all the intellectual and rational edifices which man erects to explain the universe, and its laws, pale into insignificance. Pierre's vision of the comet at the end of Volume II, his soul invigorated from his meeting with Natasha, is Tolstoy's own:

> Almost in the centre of the sky over Prechistensky Avenue, surrounded on all sides by a myriad of stars, but distinguished from them all by its closeness to the earth, its white radiance and long upraised tail, stood the huge bright comet of 1812, the same comet which, so people said, augured all kinds of horrors and the end of the world. But this bright star with its long shining tail did not awake in Pierre any sense of dread. Quite the contrary: Pierre looked at it with a sense of joy and with eyes wet from tears — at this bright star which, having covered in its parabola-like course immeasurable distances at an unbelievable speed, seemed suddenly to have become fixed in a preordained spot, like an arrow piercing the ground. It held its tail vigorously erect, shining its white light amid countless other scintillating stars. Pierre felt that this star fully reflected what was passing in the innermost depths of his softened and uplifted spirit, which was now blossoming into a new life.[9] (II.V.22)

Tolstoy's view of history

War and Peace is an historical novel. Unlike the bulk of Tolstoy's other fictional work, which tends to focus on contemporary Russia, *War and Peace* is set at the beginning of the nineteenth century and describes events which took place before the author was born — though of course a few of his older readers would have remembered or even participated in some of the incidents he records.

The background to the personal dramas of *War and Peace* is formed by the Napoleonic wars, which from the Russian point of view culminated in the French invasion of Russia in June 1812 and that invading army's forced retreat some months later. Many real historical figures appear in the novel, from the Russian Tsar Alexander I and the French Emperor Napoleon downwards, and in the pursuit of historical accuracy Tolstoy undertook a good deal of research. He read the standard Russian histories of the period, various early nineteenth-century periodicals and contemporary patriotic novels, and also numerous memoirs, diaries and letters written by those who took part in the campaigns he describes; the novelist even visited the site of the Battle of Borodino.

Yet, in spite of all this, *War and Peace* presents a rather odd view of history. One critic, Renato Poggioli, even went so far as to call Tolstoy's masterpiece 'an historical novel "debunking" history'.[10] Perhaps he should have said 'an historical novel "debunking" historians', rather than 'history', since Tolstoy does not dispute *what* happened so much as the historians' explanations of *why* it happened; Tolstoy does not argue much about historical facts, he is concerned rather to present his own idiosyncratic view of their causes.

The novelist explains his basic concern and outlines much of his view of history in the opening paragraph of Volume III of *War and Peace*. This comes almost exactly mid-way through the novel:

> From the close of the year 1811 an intensified arming and concentrating of the forces of Western Europe began, and in 1812 these forces — millions of men reckoning also those transporting and feeding the army — moved from the west eastwards to the Russian frontier, towards which since 1811 Russian forces had been similarly drawn. On the 12th of June 1812 the forces of Western Europe crossed the Russian frontier and war began, that is, an event took place opposed to human reason and to human nature. Millions of men perpetrated against one another such innumerable crimes, frauds, treacheries, thefts, forgeries, issues of false money, burglaries, incendiarisms, and murders, as in whole centuries are not recorded in the annals of all the law courts of the world, but which those who committed them did not at the time regard as being crimes.[11] (III.I.1)

Having thus characterised what might be termed the historical action, Tolstoy comes to his principal concern: 'What', he asks, 'produced this extraordinary occurrence? What were its causes?' This is the question which he continues to discuss through the rest of the opening section of Volume III, in the lengthy second epilogue to *War and Peace*, and at various other points throughout the novel. And the answer which he produces not only stands at the centre of the novelist's view of history, but also helps condition the very shape and atmosphere of *War and Peace* as a whole.

First of all, Tolstoy argues that the causes suggested by historians do not seem sufficient: 'The historians tell us with naive assurance', Tolstoy writes sarcastically, 'that its causes were the wrongs inflicted on the Duke of Oldenburg, the non-observance of the Continental System, the ambition of Napoleon, the firmness of Alexander, the mistakes of the diplomatists, and so on'.[12] None of these things, however — or even all of them put together — seemed to Tolstoy to be enough to produce the concerted movement of millions of men, the migration of whole nations.

Looking at the issue another way, Tolstoy then remarks that we cannot envisage any historical event taking place without, on the one hand, innumerable chains of preceding events stretching back into the past, or, on the other, without the extraordinarily intricate network of circumstances which exists at the time of the event itself. Thus, to take an example of a grand chain of events stretching into the past: Napoleon was a product of the circumstances which unfolded in France after the French Revolution, but then the French Revolution resulted from the state of France in 1789 and from earlier French history, but these things were themselves conditioned by still earlier events, both in France itself and in other countries, and so on *ad infinitum*.

Or, to take one of Tolstoy's many examples of a contemporary circumstance: had all Napoleon's sergeants objected to serving a second term, he says, there would have been no war. At the same time, what applies to France, to Napoleon and to Napoleon's sergeants obviously applies equally to all the other participants in the Napoleonic Wars. In other words, every historical event has not just half a dozen, not just hundreds or even thousands of causes, but thousands of millions of causes which all combine to bring about the event in question. Ultimately, therefore, according to Tolstoy, the causes of the French invasion of Russia were two-fold: (*a*) the whole of previous European history; and (*b*) the concerted action of millions of men at the time.

Now, the argument that the whole of previous European history led to the situation which prevailed in Europe in 1812 is clear, and one can easily understand Tolstoy's objections to historians who appear in his eyes to pick out, almost arbitrarily, three or four principal 'causes' and write as though those three or four events or circumstances of themselves alone produced all the catastrophic upheavals of the Napoleonic Wars.

On the other hand, even accepting Tolstoy's point that the ultimate cause of the French invasion of Russia is all previous European history, why should thousands of Frenchmen march in that particular direction at that particular moment? The usual explanations given by historians, says

Tolstoy, all rest on the concept of *power*; that is to say, historians — and most other people for that matter except Tolstoy — believe that much historical action results from the decisions and the commands of national leaders. The leader says: 'March!' and the people march — because the leader possesses what we call political power. But that, insists Tolstoy, is an illusion. There is no such thing as power in the accepted, political sense of the word; the commands of leaders do not affect historical action one whit; leaders, like everyone else, are victims of circumstances, prisoners of a gigantic web of interconnected causes. They, like the rest of us, to change the metaphor, are borne along by the tide of history, over which they have no control whatsoever. A king is only history's slave or, as Tolstoy concludes the opening section of Volume III:

> Every act of theirs, which appears to them an act of their own will, is in an historical sense involuntary; it is related to the whole course of history and is determined from the beginning of time.[13] (III.I.1.)

In *War and Peace* Tolstoy tries very hard to show that events unfolded as they did, not because of the plans, decisions and commands of the great men, that is because of political power, but fortuitously, or of their own accord. Let us consider one or two of Tolstoy's many examples of such events, great and small. First of all, take the over-all question of Napoleon's invasion of Russia:

> Throughout his reign Napoleon gave commands concerning an invasion of England and expended on no other undertaking so much time and effort, and yet during his whole reign he never once attempted to execute that design, but undertook an expedition into Russia, with which country he considered it desirable to be in alliance (a conviction he repeatedly expressed) ...[14] (Epilogue, Part II)

And this was so for Tolstoy because the first project was not part of the determined flow of history, while the second was. The invasion of Russia was fated to be; the invasion of England was not.

Next, take the burning of Moscow — which perhaps more than anything else destroyed the hopes of the French invaders. Was it planned, commanded and executed? No, says Tolstoy, it was entirely accidental, the inevitable fate of a wooden city hastily abandoned by its inhabitants.

Perhaps most strikingly, though, Tolstoy tries to support his thesis with his accounts of battles. (In *War and Peace* he devotes a great deal of attention to battles, not only because of their obvious significance in the war, but also because the battle presents a model of men acting together in an apparently organised and disciplined way.) Over and over again Tolstoy demonstrates in his descriptions of battles that the course of events runs quite independently of the plans, wishes and commands of the generals. In the first place, the site of the engagement is rarely chosen, but rather forced upon the contestants by circumstances; secondly, the opposing forces position themselves, not according to any carefully designed plan, but according to what is possible; thirdly — even more important — once fighting begins, chaos reigns. No-one can see what is going on; numerous commands are issued, but only a very few even appear to be carried out. Note part of Tolstoy's description of the Battle of Borodino. Napoleon is viewing the scene.

> Occasionally he stopped, listened to the firing, and gazed intently at the battle-field.

> But not only was it impossible to make out what was happening from where he was standing down below, or from the knoll above, on which some of his generals had taken their stand, but even from the earthworks themselves — in which by this time there were now Russian and French soldiers, alternately or together, dead, wounded, alive, frightened, or maddened — even at those earthworks themselves it was impossible to make out what was taking place. There, for several hours, amid incessant cannon and musketry fire, now Russians were seen alone, now Frenchmen alone, now infantry and now cavalry; they appeared, fired, fell, collided, not knowing what to do with one another, screamed and ran back again.[15] (III.II.33)

Finally, according to Tolstoy it is tiny, quite unforeseeable incidents which exercise a decisive effect: things like the action of Captain Tushin's battery at Schöngrabern, which carried on firing after being ordered to withdraw, or Prince Andrew's spontaneous rallying of his retreating men at Austerlitz.

Even in the chaos of battle, however, some commands certainly appear to be carried out. It sometimes happens that a general will order his cavalry to advance on the right flank, or his infantry to retreat on the left, and these movements actually take place. Naturally, Tolstoy has an explanation for this:

> Our false conception that an event is caused by a command which precedes it, is due to the fact that when the event has taken place, and out of thousands of others those few commands which were consistent with that event have been executed, we forget about the others that were not executed because they could not be.[16] (Epilogue, Part II)

That is to say, Tolstoy maintains that military commands do not produce military movements; commands and movements may occasionally coincide, but only by chance.

Tolstoy makes one further point about battles which should be mentioned here. Reports written by commanders after military engagements always give a false impression of what took place, since, says Tolstoy, the commander must pretend (perhaps even to himself) that he was in control of events; at the same time, in order to produce a coherent report, the writer must impose a certain order on what was fundamentally chaotic. (In arguing thus, Tolstoy is relying at least partly on personal experience inasmuch as he spent several months in Sebastopol during the Crimean War). And if the reports of battles written by generals are misleading, accounts by historians, who tend to rely largely on the reports of the generals, are even less reliable.

So, if power is an illusion, if leaders have no ability to influence affairs, why do armies march? Why do nations move? These things happen, so Tolstoy's theory runs, because men are subject to the same mysterious natural laws which make bees swarm. There are two sides to the life of every man, the novelist says, his individual life (*lichnaya zhizn'*) and his elemental swarm-life (*roevaya zhizn'*), and in the latter no-one has any individual control whatsoever over when the swarm moves, or where it goes. History for Tolstoy is precisely this elemental swarm-life, and historians should primarily look not at men's individual lives but for the laws which govern the swarm-life — which would mean presumably, that history should become in effect a branch of zoology.

In Tolstoy's eyes, then, history is determined, political power is an illusion, and in so far as we participate — as we must — in the universal swarm-life, we have no control over our destiny; we are completely unfree. Does this mean that none of us is ever anything more than a puppet, that none of us can ever choose what to do, that in us there is no spark of free will?

Fortunately, the position is not quite so black. As outlined above, Tolstoy distinguishes two sides to each man's life, his elemental swarm-life and his individual life. If we want to find an area of freedom, it is to the latter that we must look. In his swarm-life a man is certainly not free; in his individual life he may be. Speaking as a philosopher, Tolstoy can be no more dogmatic than that. We all feel that we take decisions and act freely, but there is no way in which we can prove that any particular actions, let alone all our actions, were not determined.

Be that as it may, this distinction which Tolstoy draws between the two sides of every man's life is central to the whole of *War and Peace*. The contrast between public activity (or the swarm life) and private activity (or individual life) is enshrined in the very title of Tolstoy's masterpiece and runs throughout the work, as the author switches attention from one side to the other in the lives of his characters, from their involvement in war to their activities in peace, from their doings in national affairs (in councils of state and on the battle-field) to their lives at home, among their families and alone with their thoughts, their hopes and their consciences. And as the novel rolls on, the contrast between the public and the private, between the swarm-life and the individual lives, grows ever more poignant, not only as the military conflict becomes more and more desperate, but also as it is increasingly born in on us that the scenes of war represent an area of universal compulsion and constraint, while the scenes of peace represent all our hopes for individual freedom and personal significance.

In conclusion, something must be said about why Tolstoy should have been so concerned with history and how his view of history fits with his general outlook on life. One important consideration to bear in mind is that throughout much of the nineteenth century most thinking Russians were passionately exercised by the question of their country's historical development. Why was Russia as she was? What was her historical mission? Should she adopt Western European ways or remain true to her native traditions? Consequently, Tolstoy's view of history may be seen, amongst other things, as a contribution — even if rather a negative one — to this particular continuing debate.

If Tolstoy's general interest in history was then only to be expected in a nineteenth-century Russian, what factors might have influenced him towards producing the particular view which he did? In the first place, he would certainly have enjoyed expressing his iconoclastic theory debunking great men. Like Bertrand Russell, who so much resembles him, Tolstoy always delighted in putting forward heretical opinions, challenging the conventional wisdom and making people sit up with a start.

Secondly, all his life he expressed a fierce contempt for bookish theorists, for men who gleaned all their ideas from books, rather than from real-life experience and their own heads. And doubtless, in his eyes, many academic historians came into that category.

Thirdly, Tolstoy's view of history reflects his fundamental anarchism. Tolstoy was never a lover of governments, states, political leaders and bureaucrats — and in his interpretation of history all these ugly authorities are reduced to nought.

Finally, perhaps most important of all, Tolstoy's view of history is consistent with the author's deep conservatism. Tolstoy did not share modern man's belief in progress and modern man's faith that we possess the ability to plan and create a better social and political future. For Tolstoy man is everywhere a part of a pattern which is far beyond his comprehension and control. Man for Tolstoy is subordinate to God, nature, history, life — call them what you will, they amount to the same thing — not their master. *War and Peace* is not a novel in praise of man's political, social and historical genius, but an assertion of faith in all those mysterious forces which shape our human destiny. In other words,

Tolstoy's view of history is as it is primarily because of the author's over-all picture of man's position in the universe. It is therefore ultimately an expression of what most people would see as some sort of religious belief.

NOTES

1. Henry James, *The Tragic Muse*, 1907-9, reprinted in *The Art of the Novel*, C. Scribner, London, 1935, p.84.
2. From a letter to Hugh Walpole of 19 May 1912 in Leon Edel (ed.), *Selected Letters of Henry James*, Rupert Hart-Davis, London, 1956, p.202.
3. From a letter to N.N. Strakhov of 23 April 1876, (L.N. Tolstoy, *Polnoe sobranie sochinenii*, vv. I-XC, Moscow, 1928-1958, LXII, pp.268-269).
4. *P.S.S.*, XII, pp.13-14.
5. *P.S.S.*, XII, p.64.
6. *P.S.S.*, X, p.278.
7. *P.S.S.*, IX, p.52.
8. *P.S.S.*, X, p.374.
9. *P.S.S.*, X, pp.374-375.
10. R. Poggioli, 'Tolstoy as Man and Artist' in R.E. Matlaw (ed.), *Tolstoy, A Collection of Critical Essays*, Prentice-Hall, New Jersey, 1967, p.22.
11. *P.S.S.*, XI, p.3. From the translation by Louise and Aylmer Maude, OUP, Oxford, 1983, p.659.
12. *P.S.S.*, XI, p.3.
13. *P.S.S.*, XI, p.7.
14. *P.S.S.*, XII, p.316.
15. *P.S.S.*, XI, p.240.
16. *P.S.S.*, XII, p.317.

FURTHER READING ON TOLSTOY

T.G.S. Cain, *Tolstoy*, Paul Elek, London, 1977.
Henry Gifford, *Tolstoy*, Oxford University Press, Oxford, 1982.
George Steiner, *Tolstoy or Dostoevsky. An Essay in Contrast*, Faber & Faber, London, 1959.

VII

CHEKHOV: THE LADY WITH THE DOG

As Chekhov lay dying in his airless hotel room in the small Black Forest resort of Badenweiler his wife placed a bag of ice on his chest to help relieve his fever. 'You don't put ice on an empty heart',[1] he said, with a wry smile. Such a remark is quintessentially Chekhovian: at once trivial and poignant, detached and self-reproachful, it helps to provide an insight into this elusive and enigmatic writer. It is the remark of a man who, while recognising the world's futilities and absurdities, is nevertheless able to laugh at them and, above all, even on the point of death, at himself; of someone, who for most of his adult life has oscillated between two professions, that of medicine and that of the artist. In its fusion of clinical diagnosis on the one hand and gentle mockery on the other, this remark can be seen in its own way as an epitome not only of Chekhov's attitude to life but also of his art.

The keynote here is one of ironic detachment, a view of the world which transcends any simple 'laughter through tears' formula and sets human beings and the lives they lead within an ambivalent and shifting framework of contrasting emotions and desires. It is a view which is reflected in Chekhov's art — in his short stories as well as his plays — in a subtle and complex interweaving of the tragic and the farcical, the visionary and the commonplace, the significant and the trivial.

At the very centre of Chekhov then, as both man and artist, there lies a paradoxical ambiguity which must make us wary of attaching particular labels to him. He himself reacted angrily whenever contemporary critics attempted to categorise him. As someone who once wrote, and almost certainly genuinely believed, that his works would all be forgotten within ten years after his death, he would no doubt have observed today's flourishing Chekhov industry — the spectacle of a whole host of biographers and critics trying to 'prove' now this thesis, now that — with a kind of amused despair.

'I regard trade-marks and labels as prejudicial', he wrote in 1888.[2] But we should remember that the nineteenth-century critic was confronted with a genuine problem when attempting to assess Chekhov. After so many writers who, from the critic's point of view at least, fell into some sort of definite category — men of the 1840s, of the 1860s, radical, liberal, conservative, populist, Slavophile, Westernist, or those such as Tolstoy or Dostoevsky who filled categories all to themselves – where was one to

81

A.P. Chekhov 1860-1904

place Chekhov? The fact that he possessed exceptional talent as a writer served only to highlight the lack of an obvious message or unambiguous viewpoint.

When the radical critic Nikolai Mikhailovsky read *The Steppe* (1888), the story which perhaps more than any other marks the turning-point in Chekhov's career, he wrote to the author with the following comment:

> Reading your story, I seemed to see a giant walking along a road without knowing where he is going or for what purpose...Write what you wish, insignificant little stories if you like, but on no account, are you to *dabble* in literature in a dilettante fashion.[3]

The implication of this remark is that any serious writer must have a clearly defined purpose, a goal for which to aim — and if he himself does not reach the end of the road, he must nevertheless signpost the way ahead sufficiently clearly for others to follow; it is the duty of a writer to act as beacon and torch-bearer. Thus, according to the radical critics of the nineteenth century, such as Mikhailovsky (as well as to the official Soviet doctrine of socialist realism), literature has a vital role to play in the development of society.

From this point of view the responsibility bore particularly heavily upon Chekhov: for he stood practically alone. By the mid-1880s the great age of Russian literature had come to an end. Dostoevsky, Goncharov and Turgenev were dead and Tolstoy, although still very much alive, was ploughing his idiosyncratic and lonely furrow, preoccupied with his own self-improvement and the establishment of a kingdom of heaven upon earth based upon his own moral precepts. And if the Golden Age of Russian literature was over, its Silver Age, the age of Symbolism and the 'World of Art' movement, was not yet born. In the political sphere, too, Chekhov's adult life straddles a period of repression and relative stagnation — the two decades between the assassination of the Great Reformer Tsar, Alexander II, in 1881 and the first Russian Revolution of 1905. The fervent radicals, the men of the 1860s and the 1870s, the bomb-throwers and the nihilists, had retired, at least temporarily, to the wings. Among intellectuals generally there was an air of pessimism, inertia and apathy. Despite the quickening tempo of industrialisation in the major cities, the bulk of this vast country remained much as it had been for centuries — 'the deep and muddy river of Russia', as Alexander Herzen once put it, 'a dumb and formless mass of baseness, obsequiousness, bestiality and envy, a formless mass which draws in and engulfs everything'[4]

Chekhov showed little interest, however, in the contemporary politicial scene; nor can his stories, with the possible exception of *Peasants* (1897), by any stretch of the imagination be termed social documentaries in the naturalistic manner. But he was too sensitive a person not to be aware of this general mood of inertia and apathy. Indeed, a recurring figure in his later stories is the more or less diseased intellectual who has become stultified by lack of will and a sense of futility. 'Why am I here?' 'What's it all for?' 'What are we to do?' 'How can I give my life meaning when all around me is so clearly meaningless?' — these are the questions which are asked, implicitly or explicitly, in story after story. Such characters are of course familiar to readers of Russian literature: the superfluous men with a long heritage stretching back to the beginning of the century. And they are familiar questions too, the cursed, fateful questions which have bedevilled Russian authors and social thinkers ever since Russia first became aware of herself as a nation.

It is only Chekhov, however, who seems to invest his superfluous heroes with such bleak hopelessness and to make them pose these fateful questions with such an air of futility, as if they and we — the readers — know that there is, and can be, no answer. The old professor Nikolai Stepanych, the hero of *A Boring Story* (1889), for example, at the end of a life devoted to science, has become paralysed by a sense of total indifference to the present, by a lack of what he himself calls 'any unifying idea' and by an agonising dread of the future — a meaningless close to an equally meaningless life. In *The Duel* (1891) Laevsky drifts around the small Black Sea resort in which the story is set, as superfluous as Lermontov's Pechorin, but emasculated and bereft of any of the qualities which set Pechorin apart: aesthetic appreciation, wit, will-power and intellectual curiosity. In *Ward No. 6* (1892) Dr Ragin, too, has convinced himself of life's meaninglessness and, like the author of *Ecclesiastes*, can see around him merely vanity and futility. He has therefore arrived at a philosophy of total indifference to everything and dies incarcerated in the mental ward of his own hospital — a fate which, although bleak, possesses a certain sense of natural justice. The narrator of *An Artist's Story* (1896) is cocooned in a dream-world of nostalgia and abstract philosophising and spends his time developing specious arguments to justify his idleness.

Often Chekhov confronts such characters with an antagonist and ideological opponent. It might be expected that these opponents, in exposing the weaknesses of these useless and pathetic individuals, would become the positive message-bearers in the stories. But Chekhov is so concerned that his stories should *not* bear any obvious messages that he makes the opponents unattractive as people, or at least vitiates the force of the points that they make. Thus, Dr Ragin's opponent in *Ward No. 6*, the irascible Gromov, has many attractive qualities, not the least of which is common sense, but he is doomed nevertheless to spend the rest of his life in a lunatic asylum. In *The Duel* Laevsky's arch-enemy, the zoologist von Koren, mercilessly attacks him as a parasite, a useless specimen who should be eradicated, but in advocating such extreme measures he himself is unmasked as a virulent and dogmatic social Darwinist. Similarly, in *An Artist's Story*, the opposing viewpoint to that of the narrator is expressed by an energetic and capable young woman, but one whose positive qualities are outweighed by her harshness and insensitivity. Chekhov's concern is clearly not so much with didactic moralising as with exploring the worlds of individuals caught up in emotional and intellectual crises and in charting the shifting sands of human experience.

Generally speaking, in these later stories, if a Chekhovian hero is aware of the world around him at all, then he is aware only of life's futility and the pointlessness, in the final analysis, of his own existence. Such heroes are clearly not devoid of feeling, compassion or sentiment, but they are hollow inside, with all the vital juices drained from them, their will-power and ability to act on their desires eaten away by the pernicious cancer of spiritual torpor.

The unaware characters, on the other hand, trace out their own paths to oblivion spurred on by pomposity, routine and a false sense of their own importance. Included here are some of the bleakest characters that Chekhov ever created: Ionych, for example, in the story of that name (1898), whose decline is charted by Chekhov with a devastatingly light and ironic touch and who allows himself to be engulfed and gradually sucked dry by the trivial banalities of life in a provincial town (one is reminded of Herzen's 'deep and muddy river'). Or Belikov, the pompous and banal anti-hero of *A Man in a Case* (1898) who is a caricature of a human being in the Gogolian manner; or the man in *Gooseberries* (1898) who lives on his estate, obsessed by the fruit which gives the story its name. In some cases such complacency, obsession with triviality, and egoism are combined with a domineering nature to produce the insufferably pompous husband in *Anna on the Neck* (1895), or the despotic wife in *The Grasshopper* (1892) who treats her hard-working and self-sacrificing husband as if he were a pet animal. The fact that the usually indulgent and sensitive Chekhov treats such characters with so little sympathy is an indication of how strongly these qualities, or anti-qualities, repelled him; it also helps to nail the lie to the widespread view of Chekhov as a writer who lacks both passion and anger.

In his Varykino notes Pasternak's Yurii Zhivago writes that, of the whole of Russian literature, he above all treasures and prizes Chekhov, together with Pushkin — for their child-like qualities of simplicity and directness. Unlike Tolstoy and Dostoevsky, with whom they are contrasted, they do not concern themselves with solving mankind's problems, with grand metaphysical questions, or with religious and social panaceas.[5] And it is perfectly true that Chekhov was more concerned with posing the question correctly — by which he meant first and foremost from an *aesthetic standpoint* — than with finding the solution. He felt indeed it was not the business of an artist to provide the solutions to life's problems:

> It seems to me that it is not the task of a writer to solve such problems as God, pessimism etc. The writer's business is to depict only those who speak about God or pessimists, and how and under what circumstances.[6]

It would be quite wrong, however, to deduce from this statement that Chekhov adopted a stance of total moral neutrality in his stories. Those who see him simply as an impartial, doctor-like figure analysing and diagnosing a particular case are seeing only a part of the whole. He is generally careful to keep a distance between himself and his subject and characters and to maintain a position of cool, ironic detachment, but the relationship is a complex one. With so many of his characters, and this is especially true of his heroes, he appears to condemn them and *at the same time* sympathise with them. In *The Duel*, for example, it is difficult for the reader not to agree with von Koren's opinion of Laevsky as a totally useless parasite. And yet this is on one plane only — an intellectual plane. For whereas von Koren is seen from the outside in a rather non-human way, Laevsky is seen from the inside as a human being despite, or rather, because of all his faults. Albeit in some ways an extreme case, he is nonetheless an indisputable example of *homo sapiens*, alive, for all his spiritual atrophy and sense of futility. (Paradoxically, he loses this life-likeness at the very moment that Chekhov turns him into a positive being at the end of the story).

It is with this emphasis on Laevsky's human attributes that the perspective shifts and changes. If a very gloomy picture of Chekhov as a writer has so far been painted, if his characters and situations, at least in his later stories, can be intensely depressing, if there do not appear to be any positive messages for mankind, or any solutions to the fateful questions, it is nevertheless impossible to agree wholeheartedly with Lev Shestov when he writes of Chekhov:

> To define his tendency in a word, I would say that Chekhov was the poet of hopelessness. Stubbornly, sadly, monotonously, during all the years of his literary activity, nearly a quarter of a century long, Chekhov was doing one thing alone: by one means or another he was killing human hopes. This is the essence of his art.[7]

This is an extreme viewpoint; the essence of Chekhov's art is not its hopelessness (or indeed its optimism, despite the claims of the majority of Soviet critics). The essence of Chekhov's art lies in the tension between these two extremes, between hope and hopelessness, between potentiality and actuality, between what could be and what is, between the idea and the reality.

These two major streams flow at different levels and different strengths during the course of Chekhov's work. Often it seems the river of hopelessness flows so strongly that we have to agree with Shestov's evaluation. The pendulum swings too far one way and we come face to face with the seemingly unqualified hopelessness of *A Boring Story* for example, or the stark horrors of *Murder* (1895). At the opposite end of the spectrum, on the other hand, there is the false optimism of the conclusion to *The Duel*, stitched on to the end of the story so that the join is clearly, and jarringly, visible.

It is my belief that Chekhov in his later plays and stories was striving, albeit subconsciously, to achieve a synthesis of these two streams: an awareness of life's futility and hopelessness, and yet *at the same time*, however paradoxical it may sound, a sense of hope. And this blending of reality with vision reaches its fullest expression in perhaps that most perfect of all his creations, *The Lady with the Dog* (1899). The two streams converge most precisely here (and also in *The Three Sisters*, written in the late summer of 1900 a few months after *The Lady with the Dog* first appeared). After these high points, the lines diverge once more and Chekhov's art ends with a rather unreal story of a young girl breaking away from her provincial background (*The Bride*) (1903); finally, in *The Cherry Orchard* (1904), the two lines disappear, parabola-like, into infinity with Gaev's hollow and hopeless dreams, and Trofimov's caricatured and equally empty optimism. All that remains is the death of Firs and the old order, and the rise of Lopakhin's commercial opportunism.

In the summer of 1899 Chekhov finally moved from his house at Melikhovo in Moscow Province to his new villa at Yalta on the Black Sea coast. *The Lady with the Dog* is the first story of this Yalta period and indeed it is his only work of fiction in which this resort is directly featured. It is a marvellously atmospheric and evocative work in which the never-ending roar of the sea, the steamships, the esplanade cafes, the late summer heat and the general air of indolence of the first two chapters form a sharply-etched contrast with the Moscow which Chekhov describes at the beginning of Chapter III:

> Back in Moscow everything was already as in winter; the stoves were heated and in the mornings, as the children were getting ready to go to school and drinking tea, it was dark and the nurse had to light the lamp for a little while. The frosts had already started. When the first snow falls and you go out on your first sleigh-ride, how wonderful it is to see the white ground and white roofs. The air is so soft and good to breathe and you remember winter as a child. The lime-trees and birch-trees, white from hoar-frost, bear a good-natured expression and are closer to your heart than any cypresses or palm-trees, and near to them you no longer yearn for the mountains or the sea.[8]

What is striking about this passage is not simply that it is clearly a cry of nostalgia from Chekhov for the city which his health prevented him from visiting in winter. It is also the sense of purity and simplicity which the first snowfall of winter brings, an expression of longing not just for Moscow but for a return to a child-like innocence, echoing the yearning of the heroine, Anna Sergeevna, for a pure and honest life, free from sin and duplicity.

The cause of Anna Sergeevna's fall from grace and innocence, Gurov, has much of the typical Chekhovian hero about him. This sceptical and casual philanderer is almost the last, for Chekhov, in a long line of amoral and predatory (but not necessarily insensitive) figures, with antecedents stretching as far back as Pushkin's Onegin. Like many of them, Gurov is attractive to women and seems to have little difficulty in gaining from them what he desires. Even the clear realisation that sooner or later any particular affair will almost inevitably cause difficulties and end in disenchantment does not prevent him from embarking on such adventures. Here, incidentally, there is more than an echo of that other amoral and rootless character — Pechorin, the hero of Lermontov's novel *A Hero of Our Time*. Pechorin, too, foresees exactly, down to the last tear-drop, the course his affairs will take, but such prescience in no way diminishes the keen thrill of the chase and the conquest.

Gurov of course lacks Pechorin's ruthlessness and hard, cutting edge. He presents a more good-natured and easy-going face to the world. He is, moreover, more constrained than Pechorin by domestic and material circumstances; and whereas for Pechorin the conquest of other people's minds and bodies is the only meaningful reality that he knows, in which it is not merely the conquest, but the intellectual curiosity that motivates it, that is important, for Gurov these affairs represent above all an escape from reality.

Soviet critics generally have attempted to show that Chekhov used the theme of escape from reality as a means of unmasking the constraints and injustice prevalent in Tsarist Russia. Hence, they argue, the imagined Utopias, the 'life will be better in two or three hundred years' time' idea which occurs so frequently in late Chekhov. And indeed, contemporary reality is so distasteful to some characters that they immerse themselves in a world of almost total fantasy, allowing the horrors of everyday life to obtrude only incidentally — Gaev in *The Cherry Orchard* is a clear example of this. It is not, however, obvious that it was Chekhov's primary intention as an artist to remove the covers from Tsarist society. He was concerned, firstly with portraying people's inability to come to terms with present reality and their propensity to side-step it by living in a more or less opaque dream-world; and secondly, with showing the need for a personal vision of life (rather than prescribed Utopias), a vision which transcends everyday material objects and which reaches into the universal, towards the ideals of truth, purity and love. Despite Chekhov's fundamentally sceptical frame of mind he nonetheless felt the inadequacy of a purely materialist philosophy, and believed, if not in the idea of a transcendent being, then at least in the existence of transcendent values. Certainly there are strong undertones of this in the passage in Chapter II where Gurov and Anna, already lovers, sit on a bench in Oreanda overlooking the sea:

> Sitting next to this young woman who looked so beautiful in the dawn light, soothed and enchanted by this fairy-land picture of sea, mountains, clouds and wide unending sky, Gurov reflected that, in essence, when you consider it, everything on this earth is beautiful, everything, that is, apart from our thoughts and actions when we forget the higher aims of existence, or our own dignity as human beings.[9]

With the forced departure of Anna, however, the atmosphere changes abruptly; the enchanted spell has been broken, and the normal flow of mundane reality reasserts itself. Gurov stands on the railway platform staring into the distance; the grasshoppers chirp and the telegraph wires hum, and he is transformed once again into the bored, predatory male, overcome by feelings of regret and melancholy. It is the end of just another affair.

This indeed is where the story itself might have ended: just one more tale of wasted lives, of fleeting moments of happiness, frustration, nostalgia and missed opportunities. And yet it is now that the story starts to flow along unexpected channels. This affair in Yalta which, back in Moscow, Gurov was prepared to regard as being no different from a score of others, takes on a new and increasing significance in his life. The memory of the episode and the vision of the woman, Anna Sergeevna, begin to dominate his thoughts to the extent that they become the only meaningful reality:

> She followed him everywhere, like a shadow, watching him. When he closed his eyes he could see her vividly, and she appeared younger, gentler and more beautiful than she really was. In the evenings she would look at him from the book-case, the fireplace, from a corner of the room. He could hear her breathing and the sweet rustle of her dress.[10]

Ironically, the very affair which Gurov had seen as a means of escape from the reality of his existence now forces him into an appalled realisation of its banality and futility. Just after the characteristically abortive piece of dialogue in which Gurov's attempts to convey his feelings about Anna are countered by a remark from an acquaintance to the effect that 'the sturgeon was a bit off' appear the following lines:

These words, so ordinary, for some reason suddenly infuriated Gurov and struck him as being humiliating and coarse. What primitive manners, what faces, what senseless nights, what dull and boring days! Crazy card-playing, gluttony, drunkenness, endless talk about one and the same thing. Such talk combined with totally unnecessary business activities take up the best part of your time and energy and in the end you are left with a stunted, humdrum existence: an idiotic way of life, from which there's no escape, just as though you're in prison or a lunatic asylum![11]

Nevertheless, despite this awareness of life's idiocy and pointlessness and this acknowledgement that there can be no lasting escape, Gurov acts decisively. He embarks on a course of action which is fundamentally different from all his previous affairs; for the first time in his life, his heart and his whole being are engaged and committed to a relationship with another person. This point alone gives the story a refreshing flavour, for the combination of committed emotion with decisive action is a rare enough occurrence in Russian literature. There is at least partly an autobiographical explanation for this of course, in that Chekhov himself while writing this story was in the process of falling in love with the actress from the Moscow Arts theatre company, Olga Knipper, who was to become his wife. But there are other, more universal considerations: Chekhov seems to be saying that people who choose to lead enclosed lives, cut off from reality, are abdicating their responsibility as human beings.

Are we to infer from this that one should act at all costs, regardless of circumstances or ethical consideration? To what extent is Chekhov concerned with the moral aspect to Gurov's adulterous relationship? In an earlier story, *On Love* (1898), the narrator, Alyokhin, faced with a similar predicament to Gurov, describes it in these terms:

I loved her dearly, profoundly but I wondered and asked myself where our love would end if we lacked the strength to fight it; it seemed improbable, but might this quiet, melancholy love of mine suddenly and rudely interrupt the happiness of her husband and children and of the entire household where I was so loved and trusted? Would this have been honest or right?[12]

We should, however, beware of drawing too many conclusions from a passage such as this. Chekhov is neither a Dostoevsky, involving himself in tortured ethical speculations, such as whether one has the right to base one's own happiness on other people's unhappiness, nor a Tolstoy preaching a gospel of correct behaviour and condemning those who transgress the immutable moral laws — as Tolstoy does, although in the case of that other Anna, Anna Karenina, it is a very qualified condemnation. Chekhov, by contrast, is saying that there are no satisfactory answers to life's problems and that all the individual can do, once he is aware of this, is to act as best he can in the circumstances, according to his own idea of what is right and what is the truth.

If acting in this way means flying in the face of conventional morality, then so be it. For it is possible to infer from *On Love* — particularly if taken in conjunction with the two stories with which it is linked, *A Man in a Case* and *Gooseberries* — that of all man's vices there is nothing more stultifying than the propensity to surrender to routine and inertia. (We remember, too, Voinitsky's bitterly ironic observation in Act I of *Uncle Vanya* that it is considered immoral to be unfaithful to an elderly husband, but not immoral to stifle within oneself one's youth, vitality and capacity to feel.[13])

Although, as we see in Chapter IV of *The Lady with the Dog*, both Gurov and Anna Sergeevna are convinced that it is fate which has brought them together, Chekhov is nonetheless clearly asserting that man possesses the ability at least partly to mould his own destiny and to challenge the apparently inevitable. This is more than simply acting on one's desire, since Gurov's innermost and newly-awakened sense of values enables him to distinguish between what is true and what is false. His commitment to Anna is an expression of his true self, as opposed to the fraudulent mask he adopts for others and for everyday existence. This is made very clear in the following very Tolstoyan passage which appears in Chapter IV:

> He had two lives: one open, which everyone who was concerned saw and knew about — a life full of conventional truth and conventional falsehood, identical to the lives of his friends and acquaintances; and the other which proceeded in secret. And by some strange, perhaps coincidental combination of circumstances everything that he found important, interesting or necessary, everything in which he was sincere and did not deceive himself, everything that constituted the innermost kernel of his being took place in secret, unknown to other people; whereas everything that was false in him, the mask he adopted to hide the truth — his job at the bank, for example, the arguments at his club, that 'inferior breed' stuff, attending anniversary parties with his wife, — all this was in the open.[14]

Yet, despite this awakening to reality, despite Gurov's positive action and emotional commitment, nothing has been solved. On the contrary: Chekhov uses the image of two migratory birds locked up in separate cages to reflect the apparent hopelessness of the lovers' situation. Any sober assessment of Gurov and Anna's future together would give them very little chance of ever realising their happiness; they are most probably doomed to spend the rest of their lives in depressing and unhappy circumstances. He will continue living in Moscow with a wife who has become irrelevant and with people with whom he is unable to share any meaningful experiences, while she will doubtless continue to live with her lackey husband in that soulless provincial town with its grey fences and second-rate orchestra. They will probably continue to meet in just such a furtive and underhand way, in just such third-class hotels, simply because there is no realistic alternative. At one and the same time, however, they are able to see reality clearly, to recognise that life is probably meaningless and absurd and certainly fraught with difficulties and problems, and yet they are also able to maintain the vision in their hearts of at least the possibility of hope.

Chekhov's concluding words are characteristically equivocal, with the two themes forming an ironic counterpoint:

> And it seemed that it wouldn't take long for a solution to be found and then a new and wonderful life would begin; and it was clear to both of them that they were still a long, long way from the end and that the most complicated and difficult part was only just beginning.[15]

Notice that the two halves of this concluding statement are not contrasted, but flow into each other to create one long, perfectly balanced sentence whose form reflects Chekhov's view that if man's mind must embrace reality, then equally his heart must be susceptible to dreams.

NOTES

1. Quoted in N.I. Gitovich, *Letopis' zhizni i tvorchestva A.P. Chekhova*, Moscow, 1955, p.817.
2. Letter to A.N. Pleshcheev of 4 October 1888 (A.P. Chekhov, *Polnoe sobranie sochinenii i pisem v tridtsati tomakh*, Moscow, 1974-1983, III (Pis'ma), p.11.)
3. See *P.S.S.*, VII (*Sochineniya*), p.634.
4. A.I. Gertsen, 'Du développement des idées révolutionnaires en Russie', *Sobranie sochinenii*, VII, Moscow, 1956, p.76.
5. Boris Pasternak, *Doktor Zhivago*, Milan, 1957, p.294.
6. Letter to A.S. Suvorin of 30 May 1888 (*P.S.S.*, II (Pis'ma), p.280).
7. L. Shestov, 'Tvorchestvo iz nichego', *Nachala i kontsy*, S-Peterburg, 1908, p.3.
8. *P.S.S.*, X (Sochineniya), pp.135-136.
9. *P.S.S.*, X, pp.133-134.
10. *P.S.S.*, X, p.136.
11. *P.S.S.*, X, p.137.
12. *P.S.S.*, X, p.72.
13. *P.S.S.*, XIII, p.68.
14. *P.S.S.*, X, p.141.
15. *P.S.S.*, X, p.143.

FURTHER READING ON CHEKHOV

J.B. Priestley, *Anton Chekhov*, International Textbook Company Limited, London, 1970.
Donald Rayfield, *Chekhov. The Evolution of his Art*, Paul Elek, London, 1975.
Virginia Llewellyn Smith, *Anton Chekhov and the Lady with the Dog*, Oxford University Press, Oxford, 1973.

RECOMMENDED TRANSLATIONS

The seven works discussed in this volume have all been translated into English in a number of different versions. No translation can be perfect and each of these versions has its faults as well as its good qualities. The recommended translations given below have been chosen firstly because of their clarity and faithfulness to the Russian text, secondly because they are currently available, and finally because of their reasonable price.

Pushkin, *The Queen of Spades; The Negro of Peter the Great; Dubrovsky; The Captain's Daughter*. Translated by Rosemary Edmonds, Penguin, 1962.

Lermontov, *A Hero of Our Time*. Translated by Paul Foote, Penguin, 1966.

Gogol, *Diary of a Madman and Other Stories*. Translated by Ronald Wilks, Penguin, 1972.

Turgenev, *Fathers and Sons*. Translated by Rosemary Edmonds, Penguin, 1970.

Dostoevsky, *Notes from Underground; The Double*. Translated by Jessie Coulson, Penguin, 1972.

Tolstoy, *War and Peace*. Translated, in 2 volumes, by Louise and Aylmer Maude, Oxford University Press, 1983.

Chekhov, *Lady with Lapdog and other Stories*. Translated by David Magarshack, Penguin, 1964.